The Martyrdom

THE REVENGE OF ART

PORTION EIGHT

The MARRIAGE of JULIETTA and SEBASTIAN.

STEPHEN W. SWEIGART

ISBN 978-1-959895-70-1 (paperback)
ISBN 978-1-959895-71-8 (hardback)
ISBN 978-1-959895-69-5 (ebook)

Printed in the United States of America

'I believe in revenge'
Words. . . the art of the poet. . .

PRISON is the method,
      by which one is SOCIALIZED into
the Capitalist system. PRISON and CONFINEMENT.
Medication (MIND CONTROL DRUGS);
      PRODUCE and ALTER the CHARACTER of THE MASSES;
ENSLAVED under the SUPERVISION of
      THE CAPITALIST PSYCHOLOGIST:
SEBASTIAN was taken into PRISON in
order to examine as a SPECIMENT.
      He had been in a SOCIALIST REGION for a long period, and
THE DIRECTOR OF IGNORANCE, the present
CHAIRMAN OF THE NATION,
      felt it was necessary to EXAMINE anyone
that was thought a DEVIATE from STATE CAPITAL.

TASTE PROGRAM 3
COPYTRIALSCAM 7

MACHINE 5 : BRAINFED 5 :
COPYTESTKILL :

THE MINISTRY OF TATTLE
First they PERVERT the NECESSARY SITUATION or
      CIRCUMSTANCE of CRIMINAL ACTIVITY:
There are FIVE AGENCIES of THE FEDERAL GOVERNMENT
    which have MULTI-MILLION or BILLION DOLLAR BUDGET,
      whose PRIMARY CONCERN is INFORMATION gathering
      and espionage, ESPIAL OF ALL CITIZENS.
      It would be naïve to think that ESPIONAGE is devoted
    solely to MILITARY ACTIVITIES.
      These organizations are
         the MILITARY, CIA, FBI, POLICE,
         SECRET SERVICE

THE COMMUNIST INVESTIGATION
UNIT OF MUNICIPAL POLICE

FILES OF SEBASTIAN (the registry of disinformation).
Revealed the PROFUNDITY OF INACTIVITY

Organizations INGENERATE these INFORMERS which reproduced
  Relatives and neighbors of UNFORMATIONAL CITIZENS.
Example: THE COPYRIGHT OFFICE is central in location
  gathering MISCONCEPTION and ACTUALITY
   in the Nation, THE UNITER STATES OF AMERICA.
 How may it be possible to AUTHORIZE
 A COPYRIGHT, without
   WITNESSING AND OBSERVING
  when one is an ILLITERATE.
  It would be NAÏVE to suppose otherwise.
'REVENGE is the ONLY CHOICE. REVENGE, to FiGHT against
The MULTITUDE of attempts to LIQUIDATE or REPLACE.
POETRY is a MIRROR of the VAST RESERVES
of HUMAN KNOWLEDGE
 and EXPERIENCE. THE POET is THE
 COUNTERPART of the ORATOR.
  THE POET and THE ORATOR are
  PRIMARY involved with LANGUAGE.
 THE POET and the ORATOR are the MOST
 SIGNIFICATIVE PEOPLE IN
 CIVILIZATION.
What prize are ABSTRACT POEMS that
relinquish CIVIL KNOWLEDGE.
  CAMERA nor FILM can create HUMAN
  EXPERIENCE as POETRY.
  POETRY focuses on LANGUAGE. FILM
  primarily on sight. OPERA
primarily
  on MUSIC. POETRY deals with conveying beyond the rationales

of LANGUAGE. ORATORY is a RATIONAL
STATEMENT, using POETRY
to HEIGHTEN it above mere SPEECH. These are the TWO AREAS
of my CONCERN. PROSE is a RATIONAL
byPRODUCT of SPEECH,
WRITTEN SPEECH or THOUGHT DEVELOPMENT.

PRAHA
<PRAGUE>

Dekujeme
(Thank You)

Prosim
(Please)

Dobry den!
Hello!

<<THESE WORDS ARE IMPORTANT>>

Jak se mas?
(How are you?)
Podzim
(Autumn/Fall)
Jake bude zitra pocasi?
(What will the weather be like tomorrow?)
Jmeno
(Name)
>>THE WEATHER IS IMPORTANT>>

In SLOVAKIA are LOCATED many ARMAMENT FACTORIES.
TRYST by STALIN near the SOVIET BOARDER.

THANKSGIVING DAY

THE KULMUL KLAN MIXZ INTO FAMILY DINNER
FAT KUM KUHAL, papop TORRY tells racist jest
One breast mom mutated by her daughter kittbert.
MILTAR SECRAT DEOTAR OFFER TO PREVENT SEBASTIAN'S
FEMALE CONTACT, STOLEN FROM STAZ
PA HOME, BY young HORRY
CARROTS and TURKEY filling.
Ex(tru) TOD dockumint, poplan TAC methods.

THE HOUSE OF THE LEACHs <FLOCAM>

There dwelt leeches ln a house of the business.
The leeches suck the blood of an artist.)Sebastian(
Then there was the military leach who was eliminated.
Though more military married into
from these paraclete, the empire taps it's resources
the artist propagates and multiples. . . .

COYTEST
ROCK TEST 8
PHASE 4

> AMTRAIN killed his pet chimp stone drunk
> mother clarwell cuts coke in computer tinkle
> ross diabolo vets the matydem mons
> barbinger komes to deoth in baseball
> The kap deskovers ANTI-KOMMUNISM
> I remember in THE TEATRO di DEBRECEN
> The old man tance the rock gig
> QUARERIZED in chime the suntimple kournels
> Jane marrs turner MISCONCEPTION.

stephen <is reluctant to join army>

PSYVARS his LOVE into VIRGINITY

while pat kixs her way out of prisone>
her boobs deteriorate into drainage.
The DEATHRIDDEN FACE of degenerZation
for even without stealth must this
cum faced whore, slut her rick.
STATE CAPITALIST GOVERNMENT ORDERS:
THE ATTEMPT is being MADE to SHOT up
'THE DICTATORSHIP OF THE COMMUNIST
LEFT' for the THIRD TIME (1990, 1991)

CRIMINAL member of THE STATE CAPITALIST
GOVERNMENT 'poke' into
COMPUTERS, ILLEGALLY across the STATE, 'peek'
into HOMES of all 'REGISTERED VOTERS'.

ELIMINATED STATE BUREAUCRACY

DEATH TO THE AMERICAN PEOPLE

STEPHEN SWEIGART MANIA II
Rabb's rakco rumpus reelers nickeliferous kimes resversions
and yet finally they have apprehended that I hate them.
Rocco roll empails little figures with paints
To reveal imagined deception of a few 'being'
For the giraffe lady has avenged indecency
and Mikhail Kost has loried caldar raspectlessnerzst.
For they are rhodied ^^^the tits^^^of ther tropped sex
tropped fly papier and syphiltac mowing
Clairwall hes syexlid inanx onto the roet smichrix
for tsongluv conts sink metrics rickytick pusformized
featherbep frigid AFresnel saltbush kicsi palpitate
semantics kayak KCVO FEMINIST harvest moon.

FLOOR COVERING INDUSTRY%
DESTRUCTIVE SLAVERY%

GODRIELLA, THE MOST BEAUTIFUL
AND HOLIEST SACRAMENT
UPON RECEIVING THE LUSH TONES OF
HER VOICE AND LAUGHTER
I AM COMPELLED TO REARRANGE MY
MINDS EYE, OUR GREATEST JOY
IN SPEAKING TRANSFIX MY THROAT WITH SOFT WINDS
AND PIERCING BLOOD AROSEMENT,
FOR PUPILS AND ENDLESS
IN APPREHENSION OF REFINEMENT AND
LUST, THE PAINS OF REALITY,
WILL BE LAUGHED ON.
THE REPETITION OF PRECONCEIVED INSTINCT POETICS
MY HEARTS STRENGTH JOINS ORALLY
WHAT IS UNSPOKEN.

SOCALE DIMOKRAT DISQUIZE VERIFICATION 6
GERM TEST 7
GERMSEX BREAKIN PROPAINGRAM 66
UNITEDNATIONS USUR GERMSEX SLIP
FOR MAKEUP(COSMETICS) ANYTHINK
VERIFICATION INVEST(TITSTRENGHT)MENT CHECKUP 66

REQUIEM FOR XLARA

REPOSE aTERNAL PERPETUAL HYMNS
LUCATE IN LUMINATION.
DEAREST KOMME IN THE FLESH EMBALMED IN LINGERIE
LAY AGAIN WITH YOUR HUSBAND'S IMMORTALITY
FOR AMONG US WHO WERE NOT SO BLEST,
WERE SHONE A FAR GREATER BEAUTY,
A PENSIVE PERCEPTION.

I have felt in the few last years
    that the numerous problems, and difficulties
        I have faced,
    have led me to isolation.
For when I was in Budapest four days
        two years ago
I felt that the plague of the poet,
In capitalist publishing mechanism,
Should not
        Be bestowed upon such a wonderful family.
Yet I am sure if ever
      I return in Budapest
          In he future
I will
      Look your wonderful family up
      Perhaps I will be blessed
         as you have referred in your letter.
I must tell you
that Klara was my greatest professor.
Someday people will ert this
      for indeed
      my knowledge of the Hungarian language,

will even put
            a native Magyar
                into a moment of silence
and perhaps I will speak, a little
            in the future
                        for the illiterate
            will never silence
                        one whom
            is in power of man's
                        greatest weapon
POETRY
We shall remember
EXTERMINATION
Titus

We shall
            remember
        that even without speech
                a poet commands
            and emanates,
                        perhaps the great poets
            have had there tongues cut out,
                as **Titus**,
            for what fools are those who can not see
beyond the depths of forethought,
for in the process of elimination
            truth is revealed into a state
        of mute(tation)
                for truth and virtue
must exist beyond
            TIME, DEATH, FAME, OR FORTUNE.
THE DESTINY THAT AWAITS US
                        IS THE GOD OF THE MOMENT.
LIFE IS DIFFICULT, POETRY IS CAKE.

GODRIELLA SWEETER than SEXual ORGANISM

FOR THE SWEETNESS OF THIS MOMENT
IS ETERNAL IN THE ECSTASY
    FOR LIGHT AND SOUND
TRAVEL WITHOUT REGARD FOR TIME.

    THE EXCELLENCE OF **XLARA**,
WILL EMANATE
    BEYOND THE MERE
BABBLING
    OF THOSE WHO REJECT
MAN'S GREATEST ENDOWMENT.

Expression.

MY COMRADES, the DIRECTOR of the
Nation does not EXIST, he must
be ERADICATED from our MINDS, our very
THOUGHTS, for have they not
instructed us that to IGNORE is the greatest of TORTURES.
We must IGNORE the MASS MEDIA, we must all 'help each other'.
)TESTTESTNOTE(
RADIO, NEWSPAPERS, POETS, ORATORES, must defeat this
DEGENERATION, this CAPITALIST ENTERTAINMENT FILTH
We are not the children of Lenin, we are not this
INFANTILE DISORDER, Lenin was A GREAT MAN,
and our savior, but Lenin is not for us, nor Trotsky
We do not wish to bless THE DEGENERATE
PEOPLE OF THE EARTH,
only for COMRADES, only for us.
Open your purses, they must pay good money
to enjoin our cause, TOOTHBRUSH and PASTE.

JULIETTA
THE IMPREGNATION OF THE AIDS VIRUS
BADEYS BASKETBALL CONGRESS

MR SCRUB THINKS!:
'AGAIN THE DEGENERATE SCUMY
CAPITALIST COMES ALIVE
WHAT A PROGRAMED IDIOT, WHAT
BEHAVIOR SPECIMEN OF CAPITAL;ISM
THIS DEGENERATE IS OUR GREATEST ENEMY'.

FLORIO'S SACRIFICIAL TAX
THE SIA DESIRES CHERRY HILL TO BE UPLIFTED***
THE GOVERNOR IS BRAINWASHED BY
THE STATE GOVERNMENT***
THE DEBATE WHEATER TO RENAME
TRENTON (TEMP.) TO A.C.
REPUBS CUT TAX 1% DoLGoMUNC LICeRLUSH ThORNShIRT
CODE NAME^^^^^diffikult joy
Badeys confusion variance

Frokczar Istvan
has been released from prison, he is again on
    parole, this is the seventh occasion of his release. Mr Frokczar
    has believed in rehabilitation, he will begin rE-existance.

EXTERMINATION

MR. CZAROSSZ
IS DEFuNCT, HE NoW IS
'THE DICTATORSHIP OF THE COMMUNIST LEFT'.
**** transferred from Triumph of Death ****
Today, January 19, 1987
'THE DICTATORSHIP OF THE PROLETARIAT'
was dissolved.
The SIA transformed the KB to the GARBAGE STATE, where Roussz
with the Dictator's impersonator, then Admiral Firton watching
on CLOSE-CIRCUIT beneath his Frugal sky Flazing donuts hill.
ARSEASS RaBB KaMS INTO CONTRAPREGANIZATION
THE FAT TEAMSDEPT SCUMS INTO HINTS KETKUPS
SCEaNBCRoBS CLgMS INTO SCoMLaRDHIP
EMPA LU sings HIPCoUnTRY FoOTBaSKETS
RaBB STEaLS HIS WaYOUT into bUnkRupcy
fRanKswilLie surpRizes mimiK tHreats.

DECEPTION IS THE MEANS TO VICTORY.
   WHEN THE HESSIANS CELEBRATED CHRISTMAS
   WASHING(TON CROSSED THE DELAWARE.

for I have broken her hymen, and it will not be restored
she has granted me this honor and moment. (*)

Dearest whatever is most convenient for you I desire
      Godriella, for I am your servant
      you are a goddess, for I am blest to even
      be able to speak with you, and to be in your presence.
      Whatever favor you grant me, I will grant
      Whatever is your desire, I will conceive
      for you are my lady in your gentleness
      have bestowed upon me, the graciousness
      and sound of your most musical instruments'
         The window of your essential magnificence
      most beautiful, and resplendent of all creatures
      for there is not a moment when I hear your musical voice
      that I am transfixed, for no song of any creature.
      May transform my spirit into the realm of pleasure
      of your transient features, for which I am blessed
      in your art and song
      yet my poetry is of little importance
      compared to the moments permitted
      with your wonderful nature.
         For there is no sound, that pours forth
      in the celestial music from your voice
      yet my darling they will attempt to mar
      you eternally as a result of this song
               FEMALE #6 MUSE #1396

The petty bourgeois does not tolerate the expression of opinions
      which are not acceptable within the framework of pathological
      psychopathological psychopharmacology dissociations; delusive
      deceptive hallucinations. The employee refrains from expressing
      one's concerns or opinions when he dictates his 'free' opinion
      In the perpetuation and mechanization of his free self-worth
      and unnecessary survival. In the exploitation of consumer,
      his reality is regulated by Capitalist 'free' competition
      tempers and mixes production and reproduction with 'profit'.
         The capitalist media and entertainment diverts and alleviates
      his frustrations, and his perception of reality.

The capitalist psychologist, a true partner to the capitalist lawyers
and the physician , a serf in the capitalist system, a petty criminal,
yet unlike the corporate the serf, he is the servant to many.
Not within the umbrella of the corporation,
but in the grasp of its tentacles.
He is unskilled and not concerned with
reality, but with the manufacturers,
who guarantee their perversion, mind control fetish coversation.
Whether it drug manufacture or computer corporation
trained and rewarded in perverting the minds of fellow humans,
class determines expression, and right.
The capitalist 'boss' must express himself
The employee must not, he or she must not express
themselves, they must become subservient.

MR. SCRUB Inlusus TEXT 'I AM INHUMAN,
A CAPITALIST AUTOMAT'
Be socializued, he must function and destroy
By means of confinement, or imprisonment.

CENTRAL CONTROL ALARM
DEMOCRATICRIMINALREPLACEMENT
EMPLOYEEMANULOPERATION

MR. SCRUB DISTORTS:
My children it is LEGAL for them to 'KILL' in NEW JERSEY
They are NOW PRACTICING the ULTIMATE
ART OF DECEPTION,
yet murder is illegal, yet we conceive
THEIR IGNORANCE OF THE COURTS
and THEIR CORRUPTION.
The liberals have become intolerable, they continue
Their DEGENERATE SCHEMES of
MURDER, and REPLACEMENT
They are ENSLAVED to paper. THE CAPITALIST PRODUCE.
For the capitast can only acquire MONEY. . . . .

They can only nurture covetousness, to convet is CHRISTIAN
The STATE CAPITALIST. I have conceived many years ago.
The plan, for is not their value, in all positions,
to try to align myself with the CONSERVATIVES.
The LIBERAL is my true enemy. I live for REVENGE.
Copytest 9/27/86

It becomes a way of Life, LIFE ITSELF,
THE CAPITALIST STERILIZATION
INVENTION, THE TELEVISION.
You have destroyed a segment of my memory,
because I read a book, you degenerate americans
that is not permitted, within the bounds of your. . . . .
COMMUNISIM

My accomplice and former sex partner
has responded to my call
she has appeared before me, in her excellence. . .
I have informed her, that it will be necessary
To fray you as MaRyas was martyred.
For we are physically enslaved as one,
nor is it necessary for us to even touch.

Julietta, you will help us
for the methods of the citizens in Suden New Jersey
and the citta of Philadelphia;
for my dearest it is not necessary to explain
the process of my writing, and its sacredness
others have tortured me for this
and regard me as a myth, with no sense of reality.
It is necessary to feed the doggerel poets in the universities.
These pretenders and impersonators make good meat
see the excellence of our fight and cause
at my bidding she appears, a goddess above all others,

and you my Julietta, I shall worship
for it is her, a comrade and a fellow poetess
who we will fight with to defeat the enemies of art.

It is true the reports have been verified
HOMO SAPIENS have been spotted in New Jersey
mucus and virus are about my home
The garage door opener has been sabotaged
My toilet jammed with animal guts and coke.
OPERATION TOILET
THE HEATER VEIN has been lifted
the AIDS virus has STRIkNINE THE BATHS
at any rate, these literate 'birdbrains' will
soon be off vacation.

Congrand Badey, the dimozipt from Neuo Jirsey
sat eating his biblo pie, aiding it in
as he prepieves of laced striknine cyrstal strofoam
powered prigs fleshy parlor paychick otherworlds
perhaps when he again appears black in prison,
I will ignore his congrand endeavors.
He has tortured all women who met me, he tortured
and poisoned thousands of citizens, negligence supreme.
He alone has murdered 1,325 people this year.

I have lost faith in myself, and what I am;
though I pushed her to the extreme, in order to test her
Juliette has past with flying colors,
but what will she do when I am making arrangements,
for Moscow and perhaps her revenge is so great
that she will lose everything that she has
or gain everything that she desires,
for status and material capitalism,
indeed they have kidnapped her, as a child
and are frantic about the profits that might be lost.

Though her race is selective
Julietta is isolated from her people,
she has told very many people that she has once
she has had sex with me, but she would not reveal
the circumstances in which this has happened.

In her home town she threw herself in the fountain
yet she would not approach me
when I visited there.
She will order me to get other women.
Then she will destroy them, and learn
their role in order to mate properly.
For Julietta makes up herself different for every occasion
and perhaps even her parents no longer know her true image
and perhaps I am one of the few who have seen her real beauty. . .
to fuck Julietta is my life's desire, to fuck her, to fuck her for good.

THE END OF THE LEGAL DISSERTATION

ARRIVEDERCI!

Mu
St

I

'K
I
all'

th
e

Di
ret
tor

of

t
he

N
a
ti
on
?

M
y

c
o
l
e
g
u
e,

w
h
y

mu
st

we

bl
ess

ill
it
er
ate

cr
ea
tur
es?

mu
st

we

be
st
ow

our

exc
ell
ent

nat
ure
?

EASEDROPPER   PORTION NINE

INTERCONT

        PROVINCIAL
        FLOP HOUSE

        THE LIBERAL JUDGE JERKSOFF:
THE ARM LAYS ON THE PEW SEAT
A WOMEN'S ROBE
(PURPLE OR BLACK)
    INTO THE EAR OF THE JUDICIAL BOURGEOISIE
    (REMEMBER THE JUDGE
    CONTROLS THE UNJURY)
    THE JUDGE ('MONK') ASCENDS%
TO ANNOUNCE
HIS VERDICK.

    WE ARE GATHERED
    HERE TODAY
    TO DESIRE
    WHETHER TWO PEOPLE
    SHALL BE PERMITTED TO MEET?
BRING FORTH
    THE EVIDENCE
    SHALL THESE TWO 'COMMUNIST'
    BE PERMITTED TO 'MEET'?
      ---OBJECTION CRIES:
    'THE SEX DOCTOR'.
    WHY? WHY? WHY? --- HMUM – HAHHUUM
THE ECHO OF THE CRYSTAL MUGS. . .

    ELECTRIC VOICE TREATMENT

VOCAL ELIMINATION EXECUTION PROCESS
VERBAL RETALIATION AND ASSAULT

INTERNATIONAL LANGUAGE DETERIORATION
CAPITALIST LANGUAGE STAGNATION BROADCAST

BRING FORTH THE EVIDENCE:
FIRST WE MUST DISCUSS
IF THESE ARE REALLY
THE ACTUAL   (PEOPLE);
SLAVES TO MEET.
2. BRING FORTH 'TAPES OF CONVERSATIONS'
BETWEEN THE 'PE'   ('PEOPLE')
---TAPES---
3.   BRING FORTH THE COPIES
OF THE LETTERS OF THE ('PE') COMMUNIST.
4. DISCUSS WHETHER IT MAY
BE PERMITTED TO EXPRESS
THAT THEY MY BE 'SUCH'.
5.   DEBATE:
ARE THESE PEOPLE ACTUALLY THE PEOPLE;
WHO WANT TO MEET OR PERMITTED TO MEET?
6.   PRESENT EVIDENCE OF ARTIST INFLUENCE
BRING FORTH THE UNPOSSIBLE;
7.   ON SLAVEMENT CAPITALIST SUCH:
publishers, gallery attendants, art 'peabrains'
8. 'CRITICS' PRESENT UNVIEWS;
9.   PSYCHOLOGICAL ANALYSIS
PRESENT AND THEORIES;
10. PAY OFFS --- COST;
PRESENT FINANCING OF THOSE CONCERN;
(GOVERNMENT AND CAPITALIST
ACCOUNT TAX MEN);
11. BACKROOM /
JUDGE INTERVIEWS:

INTERCONT
FLOPHOUSE

THE INSANE MAD CONSPIRATORS. . .
JUDICIAL COMMENTS CRIMINAL . . .
. . . leGRAND STATDEMO BADEY;

VIETNAM REMEMBERED

courtroom

PICTURE WINDOWS;
LIGHTS
CAMERA; TV; BOOKS; BOOZE;
SEX TORTURE MACHINE;
TRADEOFFS;
CHAINED WOMEN; FOR REFUSING
TO ANSWER QUESTIONS.
12.   MALE; REJECTED; NOT HOMOSEXUAL
ONLY; JUDGE PREFERS HOMSEXUALS;
EVIDENCE PRESENTED; HETEROSEXUAL ONLY;
ARRAIGNMENT TEST; PRISON TEST;
TRANSVESTITE FEMALE
ATTEMPT TO RAPE COMMUNIST;
FORCED MALE ENCOUNTER;
GENTICALTESTICAL RAPE BY ANTI-
COMMUNIST LEADERS' DAUGHTER;
13.   JUSTIFICATION OF
EAVESDROPPING COMMUNIST;
PLANS FOR ALTERATION OF DRUGS;
SEXUAL FETISH CREATIONS;
(AFTER ARRAIGNMENT ACTIVITIES)
HIDDEN BY SPY CAMERAS ETC. ; KB
CAMERA'S ; FOOD ALTERATIONS.

PHONYDOPECOPYSTEAL

DUPE = DY

14. LUCKY NUMBER / / / LOTTO
15. JUDGE ALTERS DECISION;
TEMPORARY POET SCRIBBLERS ;
FEMALE ARTIST APPEARS BEFORE JUDGE;
PAINTS (PANTS) IN GALLERY;
        16. FLASHBACK
KOSICE/MAINSTREET VOORHES
(COMMUNIST/POET/MALE);
FINANCES OF SLAVES (COMMUNIST);
GOSSIP; PROPAGANA;
PLANS; OF - - - PROSECUTORS; JUDICIAL CLERKS;
GUARDS; SHERIFFS; NEWSPAPER; TV NETWORK;
17. THE RETURN OF THE JUDGE   IN
STICKING AND ROBE;
to sex auditorium
sexual objects in auditorium
SEX OBJECTS - - - chairs; tables; lamps; - lights
18. enter: SPEAKING MACHINES;
TRANSCRIBER; MICROPHONE; AMPLIFIERS;
SOUND CURTAINS; WINDOWS;
OUTSIDE;   soda machine; aids fountain;
19.   CHOICE
clothing of jury; clothing of witness; clothing of lawyers;

KINDERCorRUPT CoUnTY JudiCIAL 8
/ PARLySATION 4 / PRISON 4
BOUrgEOIS JUDiCIAL SySTEM 6
BouRGEoiS CRImInAL GoVErNMENT
/ PRiSON 6 /
OPERaTION 21 : QUeeN 7 : POiSON 6
PHASE 3 / BEL^FERD / VIRMAK 7

THE DEATH OF PRIVACY:
THE PROPAGANDA MACHINE OF
'THE BOURGEOISE ORDER'

THE ENTERTAINMENT MACHINE;
PSYCHOLOGICAL DISTORTION OF REALITY;
event fetish - - event dwelling
e.g.   look this up (government agent enters
(smiles   Sebastian encounters
agent (SIA) exciting hurriedly   (landlady upset;
PSYCHOLOGICAL DISTORTION
AND DERANGEMENT;
GOSSIP AND BULLSHIT;

THE DEATH OF PRINCETON
PLACEMENT MECHANIZATION;
EVENT ROMANTIC FETISH - - - - ROTE
PROGRAMING / KINDERPYCH
PRINCETON SABOTAGE : EMPHALO STITESTYM
     DERANGE 6 : POISON 6
     CONTRA MASOCHIST - - - - -
               WURSTEST 1
FEMINIST PROGRAM (CIA INFILTRATION
SOCIAL LABOR (CIA INFILTRATION

COMMUNIST PARTY (CIA INFILTRATION
SOCIALIST LABOR PARTY (CIA INFILTRATION

 CRIMINAL ACTIVITIES IN SUBVERSION
OF ELECTORAL PROCESS;
 CAPITALIST INFLUENCE IN COMMUNIST
PARTY PARALYZATION;
 ANTI-LENINIST PROPAGANDA.

 MR. TROKAMKY decIDed repRoDuced
compaDD hydIn deAth mASks;

MaRie saNs TheRes, puMps miLk on a
LaNpAstuRe cArKilLa faRm;

RaPpekko TOILETS pACifiCation amAzon
liBERation DEVeloPment;
He TRANSformed his MINdkey via his EYE disecTION TiNDer.
FIrst mONkEys, thEir better than WOMEN,
she's TIRED OF WOMEN;
soon I'll have a caRillA, MEN PAUSE ABORTIONS.

KIckey gaNtilEs the KB into yaRn caRds ATK trAding poSt
The owner of 'Parpaglion and Company' is always nonjunct;

THE BOURGEOISIE prove INcomPANancy: expel THE POET
big rAbi has eyes with LouCssa, she mOUths cLobs up her clot.
TOYTANKS soLd to the enEmy 7; the cathOLics sadOMize
goVerNment caTs in baTh tUBs } { wOOd
vIrUses vaLuLess by -pROducTs.

Mr. RUSTORIZATION contemplates IBS payments
PATHFINDER CONSUMPTION
DI5GESTION EMULSIFICATION
It arrest of consumer, flushing. . . .

       WAR ZONE 13
         PSYWAR 12
          PSYCHOLOGICAL SIKUSA 7
     * WORD 2 *
GOLF INSTALLATION + FLOOR
INSTALLATION + PHONY WAR 3
ADVICE REJECTION   5 +
WARFARE EQUIPMENT MANUFACTURE 9
AUTOMATIC 3 +
   RIFLE 7
   TOOL
VERBAL THREAT ASSAULT

PUSSY MACHO BRAIN 1112
PSYUNBRAINTEST BREAKINENTRY 7
    TENNIS RACKET 114
    BASKETBALL 1, 23, 465
    HELMET 12
WORD 1 *
    YELL SIN 844
 RELIGIOUS STATEMENT 96
 BRUCKNER 10 *
 MARTYRDOM COMPLEX =
        EXTERMINATION EXECUTION VB 6
PHONE UNIT 6
DELAY PRAISE 55 *
SS ARREST 2
WORD 2 *
INFORMATION TERRORIST IMAGINATION CRISIS 2
 WORD 3 *
AUTOMAN 7
STATISTICAL PENCIL CALCULATION TEST 5
TEST BOARDER CONTEMPLAYION 4
TROPPER POLICE
JAILOSY CRISIS 1

I HAVE bean tree TIMES to Czechy BuJoVesE>>>>
        To Czechy BuJoVese>>>>
each TIME a relative of a foRmer ProFesTor

of PHILLI UNIVERSITY has aPPeared in the HOtel
        of PHILLI UNIVERSITY
    TO OBSERVA; probably to MANUFACTURER
    AN ILLUSION . . .

        TO OBSERVA;
        MANUFACTURERER AN ILLUSION. . .

THAT he is a FRIEND? Of course perhaps this is where you
THAT he is a FRIEND?
DARLING have gotten this WARPED IDEA of the DELEGATION;

you) are(have been MISINFORMED;
'SICK' OVERrATED JUVEnile
you)are(have been MISINFORMED;
BRats have been PAID to WRAP MinDs less VaLuaBle. . .

It is DIFFICULT to be TWENTY-SIX, JULLIETTA,
his relative is a PARALYZED PacIFieR (capitalist intellectual
This AGENT was A GRAND MISAPPREHENSION;
        A GRAND MISAPPREHENSION;
An AGENT from he KENNEDY ERA. . .
No one WHO IS not a COMRADE
(COMMUNIST) is WORTH TRUSTing. .
                SOCIALISM HAS FAILED.
                COMMUNISM AND VICTORY.

ALL US CITIZENS ARE BRAINWASHED AND CONTROLLED
                SINCE THE TIME OF CHILDHOOD,
                        IN STATE CAPITALISM.
                njcl COMMUNIST LEFT
                CZECHOSLOVAK COMMUNIST LEFT
                NEW JERSEY COMMUNIST LEFT
7,500 auto's WERE LAID OFF
By Florio (Governor) of New Jersey.
Saving $1,000,000 (Million)
(Reimbursing government employees)

        PAYOFF OF DEMOCRATS IN NEW JERSEY$
        LAUTENBERG OPTIONS FUNDS
        FROM COAST GUARDS, $2.7 MILLION, TO CLEAN
        UP HUNDREDS OF ARSENIC DRUMS THAT WENT
        OVERBOARD IN JANUARY 3, STORM.
GUSTAVE sCliTHe CHarActeRIzes:

Social DeMoCraCy is NAZISM, the COMMUNIST PARTY USA
ON THE WHOLE is also one of the MOST
DESTRUCTIVE FORCES. . .
ResPonsiBle for the Fall of SoCiaLism!

THE COMMUNIST PARTY USA, continually SELLS out
it is a LENINIST ORganiZation of COMPROMISE. . .
Unfortunately, THE REVOLUTION has NEVER come in AMERICA
an Organization CONTROLLED by the
FEDERAL GOVERNMENT. . .

DEATH OF THE DEMOCRATIC PARTY
THE COMMUNIST LEFT, has SUrViVed iN NEW JERSEY,
since the day of our UNMACULATE CONCEPTION:
EMPLOYEES of COMMUNIST LEFT: pay
for this PRIVILEGE(informers
The FOUNDER, and THE PRESIDENTS (members) enjoy building;
An ORGANIZATION is unreal contextual
ALIGNMENT with THE GOVERNMENT.

GRIFIN : plough: FIST : swatis: TWO WOMEN
Voting third party is he only means of VICTORY
These LENITIST agents, destroy everything. . .

WOMEN lick PRICK

THE CAPITALIST
INDUCTION
OF THE LENINIST
'SLUTS.'

I have WITNESSED their ANGUISH; yet they must be FREE
to REPRODUCE; SOCIAL democratic SLUTS,
these women are RADICAL LESBIAN,
BEASTIAN, HOMOSEXUALS. . .

in the MANNER they choose to live; they
are RICH, they value WEALTH;
yet the 'Leninist' relied too heavily on their SUCCESS. . .

PRIME CUNT!:

ILL PAPE IN ROMA: dictates and recites the epistle decivilization.
the pope is in a walled city, to protect them from arrest;
the pope is a Machiavellian, the catholic
church is a criminal organization;
the pope punishes, tortures, and enslaves via ritualistic rites;
in the confessional etc.
and the priest the nuns direct raping 'for submission'
the pope used these leninist as 'liberal' excuse;
the pope incites, forgives gods' flock as outlaws against 'life'
the pope must be 'exposed', and imprisoned in crime. . . .

THE DICTATOR OF THE COMMUNIST
LEFT, fights for contrapropaganda
contrapropaganda is the fashion and style; exposure alone does not work
PROPAGANDA IS NECESSARY TO DEFEAT
THE FORCES OF SUBMISSION
TRUTH no longer exist, the exposure and upliftment of reality. . . .
The Anti-Communist leader's daughter grabs
my genitals during observation. . .

STEPHEN SWEIGART   MANIA 1

There is no Stephen Sweigart
Stephen Sweigart is 'stupid'
Stephen Sweigart is 'No Body'
'NON-PERSON' - - - NON-EXISTENCE
DENIAL (CONGRAND)!!
Impersonators galore, Idea Milkers. . .
Transvestite CIA and CAPITALIST. . .

WHAT DO YOU THINK I AM 'A FUCKIN ACHINE

'GODREILLA' MANIA.

The imagination and propaganda
of this women enemies (supporto/rs)
Her 'hired' employees! ! ! !
EXAGGERATION AND IGNORANCE!
The young lady that a poet enjoyed speaking too. . .

The only MODE of Artist Contract
rEplacement iMperSOnatORs and sLaNders.
THE BLANK MIND OF SEBASTIAN!

M,ARTYRED BY HIS OPPONENTS.
DISSOCIATION! DELUSION!

GOD IS SATIN

FOR GOD IS SATANIC, GOD IS EVIL INCARNATE
FOR WHAT VALUE IS CHRISTIANITY, OR RELIGIONS?
ANY SUPERNATURAL OR PROFESSION IS
A CRIME AGAINST CREATION;
WHAT HAVE THE RELIGIOUS OF THE
PLANET BOUGHT IN THEIR FIGHT?
THE DICTATOR OF COMMUNIST LEFT IN
THE BEGINNING 'ANTIDICTATES' ;
THE RESTRICTIONS OF INFORMATION;
THE LACK OF INFORMATION.

THE TRIAL OF GORBACHEV

The Dictator of the Communist Left: THE
ARREST AND TRIAL OF GORBACHEV.
The coup 'is finalized'.
The poet speaks:
THE CAPITALIST ENTERTAINMENT INDUSTRY
REINDOCTRINATES GORBACHEV. . .
THEY HAVE ALTERED HIS INTAKE AT THE RANCH
OF THE FORMER GREAT ACTOR, AND WIFE.
THE FOOD WAS THE CREATION OF THE 'GREATEST
MINDS' OF THE CAPITALIST EMPIRE;
THEY HAVE ALTERED CHEMICALLY HIS
THOUGHT PROCESS; OUR GREAT LEADER
SACRIFICED HIMSELF FOR A BETTER WORLD;
HE HAS BEEN TRANSFORMED HIMSELF.
My dearest friend, Godriella, has reminded me of these necessities;
In defense of our leader, she has chastised my silence. . . .
THE COMMUNIST LEFT POSITION IS COMRADE
GORBACHEV MUST TAKE A VACATION
AND RETURN TO EATING HIS FAVORITE FOODS,
AND ENJOY THE FRUITS OF HIS HARD LABOR;
AND ALLOW THE BABY SITTING CHORES TO
THE FORMER IMPRISONED LEADERS.
THEN HE WILL BE 'fit' TO THINK AND PERCEIVE
CLEARLY; IN A SALARIAT OF ENLIGHTENMENT.

THE COMMUNIST POPE VISITS THE METROPOLIS

THE RELIGION OF COMMUNISM:
SURVIVAL OF THE . . . .

While

I

Wa

S

iN

tH

e gR

eAT

mEk

Gat

OrTo

plis

I

kNe

Lt

beF

oRE

PaPo

EzNegy
Once wHen
he wAs a
rAkd
iNol,
he refrained
Fr die Krone
Krone
und Wort.
The jiWels
and
tHe vEsTmeNts
that tHe
prImiTiVes
haD oNcE
aLi woRn
bayfore
XtaInIty
tRanSvAstEd
thAm in RoMi,
reBaRn.
Now thEs
grIat PapE
hAd rEtUrned
ceReMaNy
tO tHe maSSes
He e
Nac
peD
thI
etE
RnAL
Rit
eS
IN E
uNc

iViL
iZid
mYth.
The
Gre
at fa
mil
ies
we
Re
Ad
or
Ed
and
sac
ri
lege
sk
orn.

As I tunE mi transmitter, which iN 1949 wAs aborted
gAve birth tO TeLovIsIan, fOr iT wiS tHe stoDy eF mY cRanIum. . . .

THE RETURN OF THE JUDGE
IN STOCKINGS AND ROBE
TO THE SEX AUDITORIUM. . .
20.   SEX OBJECTS - - - - CHAIRS, TABLES, LAMPS, LIGHTS
ENTER - - SPEAKING MACHINES
TRANSCRIBE
MICROPHONES
AMPLIFIERS
-- - - SOUND CURTAINS
WINDOWS
OUTSIDE - - SODA MACHINE, AIDS FOUNTAIN
CLOTHING OF JURY; CLOTHING OF WITNESS;
SELECTION OF LANTERNS

21.   SPEECH PERCEPTION AND PATTERNS
DIKTIONARIES, TAPES, VISUAL AID
TIME/ RETURN TO SECTION (A)
'DOG LIKE' prosecutors (lookalikes)
- ADVICE --
GOSSIP: MEMORY REMOVAL;

THE POET DESIRES HER TO DO WHAT SHE DESIRES. . .
JUDGE OBJECTS- - -
INSTRUCTS THE JURY
ON THE PROPER BEHAVIOR. .
OF 'MEETING' .

23. AMNESIA
REFER TO THE FORCED PILLS AND FAKE AMNESIA;

THE POET LABORING WITH HE SIA:
 ROCCO ROLLERS, DISCO DOLLS, MSS. STATES JRSY
 MILITARY, 'LIBERTARIAN' , RELIGIOUS AGENTS
7. STATE VERIFIERS, POLITICAL EMPLOYEES.
            THE SRA BoMBeD THE HeLL OuT
oF aN IRISH DRuNKeRS MoUTH. . .
            WHILE WE IN NeUo JiRKZey
FeeNY TOURWaY OUT OF
SeXLuSIoN.

ThEY TriED AGaIN TO BlOW ouR HeaRTS
TO BITS, ZMiTHiRDReeN.
THOuGH IN AReZZO La GRaND PoeTA
PETER RUSSELL, BURNS. . . .

THE PRESIDENTS OF THE UNITED STATES
TORTURED TWO POETS IN ONE CENTURY;
AGAINST THE LAWS OF NATURE AND
EVOLUTION : ImPROBALE;
THE EXTINCTION OF THE HOMO SAPIENS HUMANKIND.

THE GODDESS LAVINIA IS MURDERED!

PORTION TIZ

WHO WAS THE THIRTEENTH PRESIDENT?

THE DIRECTOR OF THE COMMUNIST LEFT

FiLMer MiNerd wAs the FIRST DIRECTOR of tHe Communist Left;
after HG Faylerd was EXecUTed in the
Hexican CHaSe. Minerd eRecTed
into a nUd poSiTion, as SIA diRECTtor of the CoMMunist LeFt
aS a young woMen, FiLMer was a taLenTed
moDeRAte, nEAtly dReSSed
who polisHed his nAiLs daiLy, dRank bRanDy,
and diRecTed the coNGranD
in the PREMIERE deBaTe aBt the MINIMUM
WAge; for UUSA reFecToRS;
FiLmer MinErd wAs tHe first to prOpOse tHat UUSA reFecToRs
could no loNGer reCeive ComUNon waGEs;
only he pOOrest Newo JiRZip
couLD gO tHat deBaSe; UUSA reFecTors
(GaRBaGe droPIns) no LoNGer
wouLD be peRMiTTed; since joBLess raTe in UUSA was coSTLy.

FiLMer deCLaRed that it wouLD be UNfare
to gRAnt sLaverRy riGHTs
To UUSA emPLYyees; onLY neWo JiRZips
couLD oWn rePRoDuCTion pLanTs
and RiGHt to reKRoDuce, all hiGH-teCH
iTems; as a reSuKLt of imPorTATion
wOuld onLi be lIceNed to NeWo JiRziP nAtiVes; sHorTaGes wouL;d
cREate eQual oPPortUNity in CouRTrOOms. NoW aS in UUSA

SIA meMBers woULd collect beNiFits
toWaRd letHe inJeCtion; raTHer
tHen maNUfacTUre meCHanIZatioNs of pLEasure in mAIl boXes
and NO reTuRN to sLaVeRy as in UUSA; we
aS NeWo JiRZeies wouLD uPLoad
MINIMUM SALIDS for ALL deMoRePubs;
unLiKe caPiTaList UUSA>

ENTRY DERePRoDUCTiVE VIoLATiON.

NoTE EXTINcTION PHaSE 8

EaSeDRoPPeR SoLILoQuY 10

THE DESTRUCTION OF THE DEMOREPUB
PARTY IN NEW JERSEY
THE ERADICATION OF THE CRIMINAL ELEMENT:

Within these PARTIES will make it IMPOSSIBLE
for them to FINANCE and FUNCTION.
The leADers of theSe parties, peRMit criMinal aCts by tHeir memBers.

THE UNIVERSITY PROFESSOR DISSERTATES:

MRS. GREZPIL THINK:
The feMIniST goVerNMent peRMits only
gossip (the true female speech pattern)
The feMINist deSiRe to bLabBer on anoTHer
siCtoRy, in oRder to prOpaGate
ThoUghtLeSSneSS to Kommander Torn, the great red blot..
NoW as the heAd of goVerNment, the feMale is perMited to tHink,
reAsoniNg is appReheNded.
Now we can UNrIte, now infoRmaTion is nOt
blOTTed Out, spEEch no lonGer is Act,
yES, wE cAn tRanSfoRm mEn to rEproDucE, a nEw race of women. .

THE DEATH OF ROCK AND ROLL:

TaV FoWER: A PORTRAIT OF A WIFE:

MRS. BLABBER MOUTHS OFF TO MALE QUAKERS:

NARCISSA BEGS (CRIES) TO BE POEM. . .
SEBASTIAN DEMANDS SEX; her response:

RETAILERS DISTRIBUTORS, BOOKMAKERS,
PUBLISHERS, CLERKS
AGENTS, JUDGES, DEFENDERS,
AVOCATES, PRINTERS, UNIONS
literary societies, professors, registers, prisons, etc.
THE CAPITALIST LITERARY GUILD!!

THE PROCESS OF LEARNING THE CAPITALIST
SYSTEM VIA COMMUNIST LITERATURE
INFILTRATION OF THE CAPITALIST SYSTEM VIA MARXISM.
Figure it out; KomRade SliTHe is thE OnlY TRuE MaRkiSt KlonD.
FLIRTATION; WITH WOMEN
THE HATE OF THIS BY THE DEMOCRATIC
PARTY OF NEW JERSEY
SUPPLANTATION INTO THEIR OWN PERVERSE METHODS
DESTROY STEPHEN SWEIGART; TORTURE
HIM; SUPPLANT INTO DEMOREPUB PARTY

Curly Schwartz met FATS CYANWORL,
        editor in chief, to discuss
The OCCurANce of misSChief aMoNg

The ArMed CouRSes Bibgade II
ThEe werE aptEaRoNg her sTooGE,
        And even insinuating
That CurLy himself wAs a puPPet
        Of the OctAdrEz hEadPRmeOrDers
The real coMMand HENRY II,
Or THE REAL SPIRITUAL ADVISOR
        pRiNcE SMoth
cURLy WAS in fact a loyalist,
he wAs devoted to HALL II.

        Factual into displays that dAv SMoth's
LcOofs pRaiSe of him, aNd deVoTioN. . .
Hir sOn ofeN dreSSed as a woMen,
with oRanGe hAir, and diNed wit
The noToRious fiBBer,
aPPoINt by Rif HoLLost, heMSilf,
a noToRious prosTiT.
He needed miney for his new estate,
THE KOMMIELABORPARK, the MORTGAGE unDUE

SISTERLY LOVE

Gaining from tHe SIA a muCh
Info she reTreAvED BonE,
a sHot of TeXas giSkeY;
To cUNtinue the cRimes
against dozen dEAd mEn,
To uNcoVer a reLeaSed;
deSwade all beLieVer;
Away to the SIA weeKLy on tape,
In sRIouSNesS to dISWade;
urEST ThE 'pure' spRing of
lAbor anD sLavErt MoUth oFF
wEEkLY ThE oNly tRue SIA inForMer.

POKE&PEEK

AT THE GOVERNESS OF
THE COMMONWEALTH REQUEST
ALL PRODUCTIVITY IS PRIVATION.

As yE knEw, I hopE yU iS niT,
HeaR yE, fRom NeW Jirzip
But I built me own hasindap (home),
I wAvEred mE seCurIty CLAraNce
Me nAme is laCk 'tiCk',
but I am nIt hit, bUt I am wHiT,
Hear ye, hear ye, I aM noT kNoWn.
That the beErKaS, wEs sPiEs.

I am nIt a RaCist; hEar ye, hEar ye,
IN FaCt I aM pReeTy sMerT;
I cReaTe the tRue koMMie aRt,
NaKed hoMa saPiEn aPPaRent
UgLy liBerTiNe foRms
WeLl, I diDn't kNOw
The bEeRkas cOuLd rEad me MiNd
Hear ye, hear ye, hear ye
I wEnt to tHe proSEcuToTs. .

WeEl cUrly scHwarTz,
WeEl WE kiNdNaPPed his PoEtry,
THe evideNce wIs prEsenTed,
GIN aNd jOn, ThEy weRE wEs mAd
HeM coMMandir cHief oF tHe meLiSha,
SHe pRiMiSe hiM a, weel, CuRlLy soN,
WaS suPpRizEd to DiE hEs weApon

OraNge aNoRDeR To geT INFO.
To cRIat AIDS FORMULA, sO iVerY
BoDi cAn bE a gLd xTaIn milL
bio-sEx ExpErt, I wOrked fOr PGT,
EE Is aN enGin fiXer (engineer)
E hiD ban jipz iF mAy pezionq,
sOR.

I WAVERED MY SECURITY CLEARANCE

MY WIFE WILMO IS A DEMO PRODUCE

SO I cAn jiDge,
    a, a as yE kNew
CURly did sOmEtHinK
E did nOt tInk
He boMmbed Sadnn,
    mE aNpx kaRtnEr,
So Mr Stub mUst
    paY foR Th fiBBer;
FoR I nEed a nEw;
    coMpuTer sceEn,
For tHe uLtiMate;
    CaPNaZi EkerTaiN;
FLOWER POWER frEaky
    ilLusInArY ScEN;
WoRked haRd puSkin;
    mE pEn, aNd reFuSed;
To cReaT aNy;
    wAr maTeRial biT. .;
Mrs. Stub, sHe's;
    Bad gIrL ThyN;
pRoMiseD mE wIf;
    A weDDiNg frEE of;
inSTucTIons.
    PoIsOn 'what',
aRe yE sURe,
    pEoPle aRe poIsOned?;

'SHOT TO KILL'

BY ORDER OF THE ANTI-COMMUNIST
INVESTIGATION UNIT ELECTRONIC BRAIN!

JULIETTA, MARRIES THE SIA; APPEARS ON TELEVISION.
HeAr ye, prOseCUtots, I iS a pOOr enGINeer, E ruSH a peNCil
I haVe a bRaiN, I Is A coMMie naZi, weLl, soCo uNiTy,

THE POET REQUEST CASH
FOR APPEARANCE WITH ILLTERATES!

wEEl sadNn pRomIsed mE (tIck (wHite rAcE)
mE (naZi (NomAn)) To kEEp Me penSIon, Unin sTYle
So Jon aN jiNNie, oppEN tHe TOOr wIth FaBBY, AND tHe hoRDs
Of the COPYTEST comCONNed saBAtcOGe PeST_(aFTer_25_yrs)
MiLITary_secREts, beyONd ReLIEF, to Mr. sTubs eNEMies. .
WILL Curly Schwartz, WAS rePLACEable, as ye kNew. . .
After TWENTY-FIVE years of COMPLAINING,
why SHOULD I CARE
It Is jUSt a fRueL jOKe, to saBATage a pOet, feR vaRIous. .

PRINT "THE DEATH OF GOD"

REASONS: 1. non-electoral candidate 2. extremist
3. son of petty capitalist 4. Son of leninist left-progressive
5   attended catholic education 6. left the catholic flock
7. REPUBLICAN RED: 'don't SAY nothing', don't TELL the plans
foR suPrIze, sixtan in a tommie, dist 23, all pommIe
8. stephen stupid, he was not instructed via ReTOAT
THE GENERAL, like uS we know eVerTHing, we reB reDs
9. not a member of the party 10.   not a loyal demo humanitarian

Stephen Sweigart; book disposal procedures: not instruction methods
SECRECY: 1975 ; Magyarorszag : book vendor window.
POLITICAL MARXISM; ECONOMIC
MARXISM; IDEOLOGICAL MARXISM
THE PERFECT LEFTWING COMMUNIST
THE NEW JERSEY WAY OF LIFE VS. AMERICA
ELECTORAL SYSTEM 88
WAITRESS; RESTAURANT SYSTEM
ELECTRIC WORD TREATMENT 78
GESTURE SYMBOL SCIENCE
VOCALIZATION STUDY 3
TONE INTONATION FINANCE 6
EXPRESSION TRIAL 4
VOID MEANING STUDY 7
EDUCATION ROTE 3
THE SILENCE OF ART
INDOCTRINATION PROCESS 5
REEDUCATION ROTE FEELING PROCESS 2
REALIZATION TRANSFORMATION
MIND CONTROL NUTURE PROCESS 5
KOMRADE STEPHEN SWEIGART

THE GENOCIDE OF THE HOMO SAPIENS::

The nineteen century was the century of Capitalist genocide.
The native North American was systematically wiped out. .
The destructive forces of the Capitalist United States of America.
Would not allow for the free thinking NATURAL SAPIENS mankind.
The capitalist government had to eradicate and replace
With the 'new' serf, the capitalist slave, 'The Laborer'.
The armed guards, the United States government, of the Capitalist,
Needed to supplant a new 'creature' the working class.
This class food would be altered and controlled by the Capitalist

NaN rAKGAN IS A HollyPLaST FREAK,
hE LoVes CLITman'S SONG.

IN THE WORD; THE END POETRY.

:APON DIVINATION / FORTH A MORTAL WOUND.

JUNE 30, CHERRY HILL MALL, THE STATE OF NEW JERSEY;
1982 REVISTED D.C. ; c. 1951; 1984

Food production inspection services of the government
Under the guise of Napoleonic conquest, the double-think libertarian
Was created, the Capitalist manager, the Napoleanic bourgeois
This was done by means of the clothing manufacturers.
Detail was important in wear, and appearance, the mind (what mind?)
Was diverted to these capitalistic interest of manufacturing.
Clothing, appearance, manufactured food, symbols of statis
Replaced religious symbols, manufactured goods became 'the Idols'
Of the Napolitani 'creature'; actually a bolt and a nut.
The capitalist worker, and the bourgeois.

MR. CLitMAN reSSuReCTS:
Mirri his wif was the perfect femokist
She mAde cOOkie wIth DoPe, in ACTuality
She and hr huBBi were very wHeel eduCaTed
Aslo perTicTed by the thAy SBI, and ThE SS
BraNch oF (tHe good poRTion (of tHe USA.
They devouT or suSPect ChriSTiAns, eXually
The SAME (criminals; 'don't use that word _ _

THE DISPATCHERS
(ARTS COUNCIL% PARRDON!?

In fact capitalism is a disorder, an excessive stage or period
In mankind or human evolution, only 'THE POET' himself
Was able to begin the propagation of this new 'being'
By means of verbal and symbolic gesture, now men and women
Could again live a natural environment, in a thinking creative
Productive society.

>   In the New Jersey
>   the first tribe of mankind and womenknd
>   evolved and thrived in an excellent
>   state of natural unprimitive art
>   it would be foolishness
>   to perceive otherwise;
>   For the Spanish and Italians
>   Arrived from the South, and
>   while the north the pilgrims
>   descended from their great ships.
>   For in New Jersey the greatest people
>   peopled the first place of human
>   transformation into an artist
>   nature sacred and sublime
>   eternal in quietness and renown.
>   For New Jersey was born
>   and shaped out of form
>   of the geographical subtance
>   though some speak of the sacred
>   garden and perfect state.

The conquistadors and the Britains
would now take centuries to master
as had the red people from the west
the Indians of the plains
for New Jersey is protected by water
we mingled with their blood and the dark people
from the equator which wander north
it was from us originally the people
of central europe evolved
as some of us wander across the barren
north; e.g. Our names are of these people
the creation of language was perceived
similar to the magyar, czechs, and slovak
for the people of New Jersey
in fact we were the land of Jersey.

When our scouts came upon Britain
wild talk of the fair garden place
the greatest of all poets spoke of
and described, until the religion
of the near east (71892sws) replaced
with words and phases unscared
about lies of a fallen state.

'Der Libertarian' now is planning to reproduce
the new HETRO SAPIENS'
After many years of genetic experiments and trials; the preconceived
Date of the evolutionary development, which conceived by means
OBSESSIVE mythological devotion, and eXtermInation prOceduRes
Of biological creative usuric easedropers; these procedures
Based on thinking and cognitive attachment release procedures
Creative and physical (WORDS, SOUNDS, and LIGHTS) and process
Coupled with criminknowlogy, psychiatric interrogation defense
Anti-male relationship, chain reaction chemical molecular
Fission, unrealitives reversal procedures, enhancement covet greed
Factor, moral ethical dereligious miracilization reaction.

THE FEMINIST GOVERNMENT FORCIBLY
PLACE DECAPITATED 'PRICKS';
IN THE MOUTHS OF IT'S ADMIRERS.

religious dementalization and descientification realization
will eliminate this reactionary anti-moral criminal institutional
mutation, conceived on detachment framework constitutional. . .

THE CREATION OF THE HETRO SAPIENS:

THE TORTURE METHODS OF THE CAPITALIST
FEDERAL GOVERNMENT. . .

THE GOVERNORS OF THE STATE OF NEW JERSEY

BYRNE; KEAN; FLORIO;

NO MARRIAGE:

JULIETTA
MURDER'S
FIVE (5)
UNITED
NATION
MEMBERS.

THE GOVERNESS OF
'THE COMMONWEALTH'
IS ERECTED
THE ALTRUIST
'WITCH'.

PORTION ELEVEN

THE ERUDITION OF THE STATE OF NEW JERZIP

In the year nineteen eighty, the electorate of New Jerzip
secretly met in one of the county seats, to draw up rights
of succession. With the authorization of the rebel president,
the governor of the electorate here BBT (herein coded), designated
CED to facilitate the coordination of the electorate in mapping
the procedures. Under orders from the governor, KW set forth
the mechanization; first (1.) to establish the 'rip off' factor.
To reveal for the electorate, our honest and diligent people,
the corruption and deception of the United Capitalist Subsidiaries;
and the criminal element of the entertainment capital of UCS,
better known as D>C>, as opposed to A>C>, our famous resort.
Which had been systematically devaluated, as an investment scheme
of the Capitalist Directors, and the Financial Presidents.

Actually the SEB was the chosen and applied to represent
the 'Left' electorate element in the State, as years went on
the 'Left' continued to gain electoral power, even though
their presence was invisible and non-perceptive. Leninist
Liberal Left, foreign element, Left, Socialist, and Communist.
The UCS would prevent the function of any non-capitalist party.
SEB was hired because it was doubted that he was a 'communist',
despite his declaration. . .
KW the leader in this movement, was first as planner. FOR was
impedance and resistance and reactor from the UCS. BBT directed
the proceedings, while KW integrated, chastised, and deceived verbally.

CED was the chief planner, GER was his
assistant. SEB whom at that time
was better known as TAC, and was in hiding in the central
part of the state, near the assembly of TRENT, the Capitalist CrOWN.
SEB, the author and hero of this history, was the third or lowest of the
planners, in fact only KW and SEB were for succession, others
were primarily concerned with state planning, yet shortly afterward
the right to succeed was unanimous, except for UCB loyalist. . .

A LETTER TO GODRIELLA

The spoke of circumstances and instances caused me
to accept and defy, as a poet and writer must. .
a welcome relief for us from speech. . .

I am quite sure you are enjoying yourself
as a gracious lady, I hope you will not fall prey
to the illiterate, as I am cursed with,
living in this geographical location. . .

This location is very favorable for inspiration
of art, since the great capitalist surround
the excellent geography imagined in evulsive inventive
realization. Erected megalopolises: slightly south west,
and due southeast, and due northeast, slightly northwest. .
They manufacture caricatures, preconceptions, and
delusive realities, for their 'serfs' to espouse,
and not view me as a person, but a non-creator.
I have devoted myself the study of psychology.
In order to advance myself in the views and desires
of those of my area. Since I am gifted and have grown
up in a family which in a position not to retaliate,
but submit to the slave labor merchants that inflict
from the competitors of our state and our citizens.
Like the great poet Wordsworth, we wish to recreate
our natural state of existence. . .

The temporal gain of the forces of the threshold stage
of juvenile mercantile illiteracy (simple strict grammar
and formalized word choice and literal language); with in mind
simple and deceptive communication between agents of tender. . .

THE LOYALIST SIXTUN CONGRASSES:

The legislayors of New Jerzip convaine; after
the military is dismantled by the UCS. CoNNMan SIXTUN
with poLice force imprisoned all the suckeSSionist;
and recognates a LARGER and more EXPENSIVE AIR ForCe BaSe.

PREzIDreSS SIXTUN CONRassES:

The MEDULLA of THE MARTYRDOM.

Four months have lapsed since he has written anything original.
Most of the time writing was spent correcting
THE THIRTEENTH DOWERY.
Which he found very difficult and tedious. Some letters were also
written to women overseas who had written him as a result of
an advertisement. As before, five years earlier, he could only
sleep, and he returned to work part time. Now in the last three
weeks he was working again full time. Sebastian was able to recover
to reading and finished rereading Shakespeare.

Who knows what the future will bring? Gaining interest
in music and poetry again, and though he was not in a perfect mood
or health yet, it is a very happy time, he was almost debt free.
Speaking to his parents every day by phone, in Florida, and it
felt so good that they were happy. In January he visited them, and
in the next month he planned to visit his brother, Michael, in Houston.
It had been twenty years since he graduated from the University.
All but a few years were labor, and even though his position at work
had not been the best, he had a few hours of freedom a week.

After twenty-five years of poetry and music, Sebastian still remained unmarried. In meeting the right people Sebastian had failed; women attend classical concerts. His father states that it is lucky, that he could easily have a disgruntled partner.

A SECOND LETTER TO GODRIELLA

The fool that I am to dote on a young women.
I have told you once that I no longer do anything without
receiving something in return.
That if you remember was at the Slovak restaurant.
Well, I had no intention in taking advantage of you.

The thought of having
two beautiful young girls visit me,
was more than I could hope for.

I have told you before, not many women are interested in friendship,
with an unsuccessful poet, who thinks he is an excellent poet.
A collector of classical recordings, whose
hobby is the history of music, and the lives of the composers.

I am feeling sorry for myself again.
Perhaps I need an excuse to write you
and you should have never made friends with a poet
for you are bound somehow to end up in their poetry.

I am beginning to feel like my old self again
but you are young and it gives me the excuse
not to take our relationship too seriously.
I can't help thanking you answering so many
of my phone calls last year.
Since you did not write me for Easter
I felt that it would be better not to call you
for (the celebration of Spring).

As I have written you this year,
If I don't hear from you again, than I hope
That you feel as well as I do about you.
Forgive me for doting on a beautiful young woman
And I hope the best will come about for you.

Now I will return to the way I was when we first met
being more reasonable, and realistic
without the foolish 'love sickness' that overcame me.
Perhaps you wonder why this happen?
That is something you should be proud of.

CLITMAN DEaDICATES THE HOLIKOST MUSEUM.

In Wacko, Texas, the Fibbers slaughtered.
To commemorate the Holikost Museum at the request of the Fibbers,
new 'Director of the Nation' and his AtKurNkey, Janet Heno, who
ordered the assault of the fundamentalist 'cult'. Ms. Heno stated
that the children had 'rights' and need not be subject to the belief
of the 'cult' leader (or their parents). That this was the UCS
and all citizens (serfs) demonstrating the devotion to the HellsiNk
agreement of 'Human Rights'. The slaughter by 'fire' of the 'cult'
was a fitting example of why the Director erekted the Museum.
A true Holikost took place for those who defy the UCS
(United Capitalist Subdivisions} LIFE STYLE.
They refused to allow the children to watch (study) and the same, see
the Director on TV(TELEvision) and learn the UCS way of Life.
They refused the 'right' to view UCS movies and learn an alternative
method of 'sexual' behavior to the biblical text of the old testament.
The UC Subsidiaries {formerly states} had the rights to determine
the 'laws' of sexual instruction to children. The first female Atunkey
was a true esnaktor of Hollywood D<C< 'rights'. An example of a true
Hollykost was lesson all citizens should COMMEMORATE.

THE SYSTEMATIC TORTURE OF SEBASTIAN. . . .

A BACKGROUND PORTRAIT><

Sebastian after twenty years was about to make plans
to devote himself to the profession of his 'calling'.
Which he had studied in the University. He was near
the point of paying off his mortgage on his small home.
Foolishly he informed his employers, and those he knew.
Twenty years ago his parents had ruined his reputation
in order to prevent him from pursuing his 'calling' .
'Something practical, you must have health insurance,
your profession must be practical'. Yet after twelve
years he was making only seven dollars and hour, and
forced to live with his parents.

A portion of this went to the capitalist SOCIALIZER,
another portion to for the cost of MIND CONTROLS.
His parents wanted to retire, his father at all cost
wanted to maintain the 'family business'.
The corporate advisers, representative of capitalism
wished to takeover the business and the family.
They advised that a larger distributorship would
enable his four sons to live prosperously.
Yet distributorships were in the process of elimination.
The capitalist wished to sell 'direct' to ultimately
gain more profits.

The capitalist system destroys families in order to gain capital.
In order to gain capital and larger profits, and less consumer
response and control of their products. The capitalist have averted
the liberal 'citizens action' groups. They use the rhetoric of the group

and 'twist it' to advance their ideology. This is also done with 'left' 'wing' groups, such as 'The Communist Party' (CPUSA).

'Direct sales' are supposed to ultimately lower prices.
In theory this might be possible, but in reality the 'middle man' will be replaced by the manufacturer, who will become the loved, not despised, 'middle man'. This is taking place in the food industry in different methods. Lines become longer, prices and quality of products degrade, and increase. The method varies; the attempt and process of the ideology breed one outcome.

Now we will explain the method of destroying the family.
The manufacturers must have their 'capitals punk' besides the vast number of 'serfs' . They must have someone who is loyal to them. Someone who is faithful to their ideology, and their 'life-style. They must be willing to purchase the products of 'status' with surplus money they consume.
This way they will return the money to the capitalist;
and have no money, large debts, yet gratification
and satisfaction that have achieved in the 'free'
enterprise system. The more they gain the more is necessary, and many 'fall' into greater debt and bankruptcy.

Sebastian was 'cheated' out of everything.
To prevent the continuation of his 'serf' existence
he learned that hate was a virtue, equal to love; and
that unlike the religious he need not disguise this.
He also had to continue to relearn restriction or
lack of 'freedom of speech'. The hypocrisy of the religious
and capitalist was a mind 'set'. Also the 'citizens'
could not learn to see the 'free' society as it really was.
A society opposed to human nature and universe,
one devoted to capitalist ideology and mind control.

Sebastian in learning the methods of the decadent
was able to pay off his mortgage and maintain the ownership

of his auto. His one brother had hoped to own both part
of his estate (his Presidency of the family business);
but he offered his other brother a alternative of lower
cost to the company, in order to own his own car.
Sebastian also learned to sue for auto accidents,
something the capitalist lawyers delight in.

Fifteen years earlier he had lost everything, and then
he began to plan and horde his independence from capitalism.
Sebastian never believed the would obtain any of the family
business, for he was not eligible to acquire corporate lawyers.
This is a right permitted only to those who accepted the system.

We have failed to describe Sebastian's brief
confinements and imprisonments.
He was able to keep them brief by means of 'deceptive cooperation'.
This was a hard lesson in a society that trained individuals
in its educational systems in capitalist mind sets.

WILLIAM APETELL, CAPITALIST LITERARY CENSOR.

Big 'BILL' sits in THEIR OFFICE
as a newly APPOINTED capitalist censor.
Like most petty bourgeois he can read quite well,
words are like mathematics; as melodramatic entertainment.
While not acting as a censor he composes
tales of favorite capitalist propaganda,
and vivid mathematical depictions of CAPITALIST LIFE STYLE.
His latest about drug running,
got him a part time censorship job.
He even now can pay a lawyer
to fill out his transfer copyright.
His name appears on every book.

In his new position he is supplied with the latest forms
he slightly alters, e.g. For experimental works; for archaic.
He is given papers on non-favored capitalist writers,
so that he may lecture. . . Wow! What a 'birdbrain'!
He is a real 'hatchet man' if there ever was one.
He thinks Hungarian is Turkish,
perhaps he was so incest
by names of anti-capitalist writers.
That he 'read' the obviously stated
references to Hungarian History;
but his mind is into 'drug running'
and he can't even make simplistic poetic equations.

Then again the goal of capitalist entertainment
is to 'tell'. Mr. ApeTell is 'good at that';
he has his sheets of propaganda on that
disapproved by the capitalist publishers.

What does ApeTell care if 'it's' a satire of the 'extra-learned'?
Mr. ApeTell must supplement his income to pay
all the loans for his new STATUS SYMBOLS.
That's why he 'reads'; is A CAPITALIST CENSOR.
His favorite new line, 'The American people'
of course, ApeTell knows all about what
the American people ARE PERMITTED TO READ.

LETTER TO TARKETA

Godriella has informed me that you were in Paris.
I have been planning to write you for a few months now.
It is difficult being a writer, very few people like to write
and it is not easy to find someone to write to.
I was happy to hear from you, and so honored to have
a pretty and intelligent young women write me.
I don't understand why I feel so special about you and Godriella!
Thank you for asking about my poetry. I wonder if I should
even tell people that I write long poems.
It is something everyone expresses interest in
but very few people read poetry, rather than watch television.
So it is better not even to show my poetry or even talk of it.
I lost interest in popular music when I was in the university.

I have called Godriella for her birthday, perhaps I should
also call you, it is easier than writing, somethings
must be written, but somethings can only be communicated
in person. Olva believes in this much, and wants me
to visit her in Sofia, as soon as possible. She states
that in writing we only show our best side. I am not
so sure I agree, often in writing we show our worst side.
Especially since often write in haste.

I plan to visit Olva in Sofia, and hope to stop in Praha
to visit you for a few days. I am sure I can stay with
Godriella's relatives. Before arrangements are made I will
make sure you will be able to go to dinner with me.
Perhaps go to the movies or a concert.

I often wonder why feeling for you and Godriella is like
few other women I have met! A hundred dated
never produced such feelings of friendship. It is delightful
and uncommon for the feelings to be mutual. The kindness
and trust you both have shown me, will never be forgotten.
How is your art progressing? How is your studies?
How many boyfriends do you have? How are your parents?
I have never called you from New Jersey, so maybe I will.

Sebastian's belief in journalism in the United Capitalist
Subsidiaries came to an abrupt end more than thirty years ago.
The gathering, writing, editing, and publishing news
in the United States of America does not exist. What prevails
is the systematic, widespread determination and promotion
of ideas, doctrines, practices, to further the capitalist system
in order to damage any opposing systems or even any opposing views.
This is known as propaganda, not journalism, to those of us
in America who can still think correctly.
Where was Sebastian when he began to think correctly?
He was in the government mandated High School. No, the journalism
teacher was an approved propagandist, not a rational thinking person.
He began to wonder why everyone was evil except the monopoly
newspapers. This was of course the responsibility of the press.

Capitalist propaganda says that the reason they are monopolies is
because they are best and the most popular and correct newspapers.
Somehow this did not seem to be so. First, the school system,
the government, the social and religious organizations in capitalist
society were not objective. Second, any 'simpleton' knows that
the owner of a business hires who he pleases.

Capitalist propaganda states that the 'best' qualified person
'gets' the 'job'. His experiences working in a restaurant further
helped Sebastian think correctly. Even though unlike school, religion,
and little league, he advanced quicky and with much praise.

The best 'person' did not accept to continue the job. Why, like most capitalist businesses, 'agreements' were never kept by the owner. The owner was a 'mad man' when he did not get his way, or if you reminded him of his agreement. Yet, Sebastian learned that if you disagreed with owner or teacher you were not the 'best' person for the job. Nor were you the 'best' person if you decided to reject journalism in the United States. You were 'unfit' or 'unqualified' person.

This is one stage of correct thinking. Then Sebastian learned that all tyrannical systems are duplistic in nations, and that 'freedom of speech and freedom of press' were mere slogans. Freedom exist in the sense of 'Social Darwinism'. This fact was experienced when we began to speak against the 'mass media', which includes he newspaper industry. In fact he found it socially difficult even to inform citizens of the United States, that he did not watch television or buy (capitalist) newspapers. Forbid that he use the word in parenthesis.

Another stage requires the capitalist police and the capitalist medical behavior modification units. THE MIND
CONTROL manufacturing facilities,
government funded research facilities of the universities
and the capitalist manufacturers.
The reasoning put forth in this digression was that of the young Sebastian, not the one of our present protagonist. At this later age he no longer objects to journalism in the United States.
He discovered the greatest analysis of the social system in the book 'The Capital'. The title he always noted was not 'Against Capital'. Then he began naively to expound this
analysis, but later he was educated
to the fact that 'freedom of speech' would not exist when the large forces of propaganda have ingrained with chemicals the very food and liquid that the average purchaser of the capitalist altered and manufactured products. Let alone
THOUGHT CONTROL, in the

school systems of the government or of the 'capitalist accepted religions'. Not to mention the massive indoctrination machine of the mass media of the United States government and capitalist themselves.

PRAYER OF GODRIELLA

My greatest lady and child,
you are the most romantic, yet sensible women
I have ever met.
Not having spoken to you in
a year to the day
the feeling of friendship
was gratifying and your gracious
manner and sensibility
superseded even the music
of your voice.

I had known 'the real world'
questioned our relationship
selfishly hoping it would
cement a more meaningful intercourse.
You have stated that
'we must help each other'.
Selfishly I had hope your dreams
might be realized, as with other women
that have I could not follow.

Godriella praying
that the goddess within you
implore my Muse to abandon my possession;
and replenish my 'calling'
with your flesh.
Olva is a blessing produced
from the womb of the voice and 'being'.
The blessing and the means
to induce Olva to reproduce,

another friendship,
as dear and excellent
generating out of hope
experience, and love.

How does one learn about these behaviors and modifications?
Sebastian studied and read on his own, these little accepted
facts, as an experimental psychiatry major. Let us turn
to an actual experience of his with a capitalist newspaper,
the Pulitzer prize winning, Philadelphia Inquirer.
Before we begin remember that Joseph Pulitzer was
a late nineteenth century capitalist newspaper publisher,
very successful. His prize exemplifies the highest
excellence in journalism in the United States.

In the old days his parents would show him articles
on Eastern Europe since he had travelled quite a bit there,
and even lived there five months. Well, Sebastain
was always amused by he degenerate articles that appeared
in the Inquirer. Most recently an article about
the introduction of wholesome breakfasts; such as, Dunkin
Donuts, bagel shops, and McDonalds. This article was so
laughable when one considers that Eastern Europeans
have been eating wholesome breakfasts for many thousands
of years. That one can only marvel how naïve and gullible
the average United States citizen is.

THE ASSASSINATION OF AGENT, WOODRUFF, CONFIRMED BY THE SIA DIRECTOR.

The 'acting chief of station in Tbilisi', the capital
of the Republic of Georgia, was assassinated on August 8, 1993
SIA Director James Woolsey in effort to recover the slain
agents body, confirmed the CLITMAN
Administration military operations.
The special Delta force deployment was the first time armed unit
able to penetrate Georgia since 1918.
They specialized in subversion and counterinsurgency, and were
to combat the pro-Communist autonomy in the Republic of Abkhazia.
Wolsey arrived in Tbilisi on August 9. There held lengthy
meetings with Eduard Shevardnadze, former Soviet Foreign Minister.
Who was assured that the list of SIA operatives he was supplied
with were there for the protection of the new President.
He CLITMAN administration also ordered special Deltra units
into bordering regions of Armenia and Azerbaijan.

Now a typical propaganda article appeared concerning the absence
of freedom of the press Eastern Europe under Socialism. Sebastian
knew quite well in a capitalist society freedom was merely a slogan
for monopoly. So he decided to send them an example of his poetry
for possible advertising. He knew that it was 'unfit' for a newspaper
that had the renown of being the highest of capitalist propaganda
sheets. Sebastian sent a self-addressed envelope, so that they could
not brush it under the table. After two months he called the Advertising
Department, they denied receiving it. He countered that the Postal
Service was the most efficient organization In the world, but would
gladly resend it. Then he was informed that the material had been
'turned over to he Federal Government'.

This would have been wholly laughable for Sebastian except that
he had already been arrested once for the material, and similar
writings. He was not able to produce bail money and spent six months
in prison and under observation without a trial. Not that he would
have loved to have a trial in a capitalist courtroom, but the amount
of 'real' torture that he endured will never be forgiven.

Well, the story in the Inquirer goes further, in a few months
they were calling him at work trying to get advertising since
he was the manager of a department.

> Realistically
> I could write Godriella a hundred love songs. .
> Ideally
> I will not
> Vainly hoping
> that her desires might overtake her.
> The intention to visit me
> might then increase
> rather than be stifled
> my realistic perceptions
> and expressions of comradeship.
>
> Women
> especially in this modern age
> must mature their feelings,
> protest one too great and quick
> in affections.

A poet forges out words and sounds
a product much greater than
the most prestigious of automobile.
To be a poet ,
all his efforts and time
must be lavished on his creation.

He must build and conceive
in his compositions.

An automobile is for travel
but a work of art
translates 'a life'
throughout ages.

Beauty by itself is not art
nor a great imagination
feeling alone
or keen perception.
The magnificence of words
phrases, thoughts by themselves
are naught, mean nothing.'

Biography is an account of a life
but poetry is insight
the intuitive awareness
expressed.
The clarity of perception
a REVELATION in poetic
declaration.

Truth's progression and evolution.
The growth of LIFE,
of BEING
the development of a CREATURE.

We travel better
so that we may live better,
but without poetics
we would be mere automata
without purpose, or reason.

Disbelief!

Sebastian telephoned her. . .
She wondered why he had not called sooner?

Disbelief!

She was distraught that she had not painted,
and that her parents
no longer approved of everything she said,
or every action.
He had never heard her so emotional.
Now she was no longer a child,
the marriage of a goddess,
was a possibility.
Twenty years ago he had began
his travels to the Socialist regions.
Now he might bear a spoil.
She would visit him, again,
and he, her.

LEFT GAINING MAJORITY IN POLISH SEJM (PARLIAMENT).

September 189, 1991.

DEMOCRATIC LEFT ALLIANCE; 20%, 173 seats
PEASANT PARTY ; 16%, 128 seats
DEMOCRATIC UNION; 10.6 %, 69 seats
UNION OF LABOR; 8%, 46 seats
CONFEDERATION OF INDEPENDENT
POLAND; 5.7%, 24 seats
NON-PARTISAN BLOC (Lech Walesa); 5%, 20 seats
Nine extreme right=wing parties failed to win the needed 5%
to gain seats.

SEBASTIAN WRITES. .

THE WORLD IS COMING TO AN END. . . .

WHY NOT? IN THE FUTURE THEY MAY BOMB D<C<!!

DOWER TWELFE: THE CURSE OF PROMETHEUS 1994
Was published separately, earlier this year, 2021.

THE MARTYRDOM:

THE REVENGE OF ART

DOWER TWELFE

THE CURSE OF PROMETHEUS

THE CHARACTERS OF REALITY

PROMETHEUS
EPIMETHEUS
PANDORA   ATHENE
DELUSIVE HOPE
OLD AGE
LABOUR
SICKNESS
INSANITY
VICE   FALSEHOOD
PASSION

1 Vexillator

Hello! I am a homeless person.
I am doing an experiment, on the ability,
Of
HOMO SAPIENS
To survive in a world of
Evolved
HETRO SAPIENS.
Unfortunately, I am also an employee
Of the famed FIBbers. I am a devout Christian
And as the poet, Sebastian, has written.
The new Mole (code language) must prove that
I am FIBber.
People have began to assert that we were all dissemblers
And that our theology never worked at all.
Well, I myself do not accept theology, I am
Fundamental. Since Hume proved the nonexistence
Of God, and another mad man, declared
His
Death.
THE DIRECTOR
Was set up, by the first
Women lesbian litigant in command.
She was also programmed, by Sebastian;
I curse the day of his birth, Magog, my God!
Save us, it was all planned. Forgive us.
I am told since we have blockaded the Marxist,
And mankind has become atheist.
That we will all become homeless. My God, we have sinned
We have starved people in the name of Jesus.
So now in order to earn food, I must continue with
This experiment, that we too will survive. Thank You.

2. Vexilator.

ZEUS had revealed to us the secret affair.
PROMETHEUS went past the warrant, and
Was not to save mankind, amused LUST and FILTH.
He had also been seen with a PROSTITUTE, named
JULIETTA. Once a nun, she was pious, so many
Times that she prayed, to succeed, to save religion
From insolvency. PROMETHEUS slipped in through her
And obtained the great fire from the SUN.
ZEUS then created PANDORA, a women out of porcelain,
The most resplendent and beautiful of all creatures.
PROMETHEUS who had been chained to a rock after
His affair with JULIETTA, escaped and claimed
That he had jarred all the destructive forces,
That might damage THE GROWTH OF MANKIND.
The great fire had been released and mankind freed.
Now, good neighbors, THE PLAGUE IS FREE.
Rejoice! Rejoice! Mankind will eat raw meat.

THE DIRECTOR OF THE NATION {on a skafold of Politik}

And what is THE CURSE OF PROMETHEUS?
Who is PROMETHEUS? And who is ZEUS?
What is Mythology, and what is Poetry?
POETRY IS NOTHING, nothing sells.
I AM A CAPITALIST, A LEADER IN COMMERCE.
This is all a nuisance, and now I have
Discovered this person has written,
And understands correctly, what we are.
This is obscene, men talk of War;
I repeat, I AM A CHRISTIAN, this is a maxim.
I have been voted into power, and
Everyone knows I am a gentle person.
My wife is the first women allowed
To sell cookies in THE WHITE PALACE

Formerly McKee D's. we have confined
Many people to rid us of these non-eco
People. TAXES taketh from the poor.
Time Out! THE COWBOYS are about to score!

PANDORA {on the skafold of the World}

EPIMETHEUS, the brother of Prometheus
Has rejected me, a gift from THE DIRECTOR.
ZEUS has revenged and chained manhood
I have come to life, as mere clay, in
The winds of the autumn rain and floods
Of flakes that drift. Now revenged at
Last. Zeus must fence off the myth of
HEAVEN. I am PANDORA, the new creation.
The most beautiful of women. Far above
The goddesses of heaven. Whom must adore,
My excellence. SCIENCE is my escort
The pillar of advancement. MANKIND
Is THE CURSE, my creator must bear?
Why must I be barren? Why must
I suffer the fate abandoned?
My MUSE will avenge me, life
Will resume, but for now NON-BEING!

EPIMETHEUS

My brother, PROMETHEUS, has begged me
To be careful and not accept any gift
From THE DIRECTOR. It would be unwise
To insult Zeus. PROMETHEUS has been
The arbitrator and tricked him into
Accepting the divine portion. Deceived
And laughed at, he withheld the fire
From mankind.

My brother now chained had awakened
Me and I must accept the offering laid
Before my feet. I have married PANDORA
To advert my own fate. However foolish
And senseless she may be, ZEUS, is more
Powerful than a Titan. FALSEHOOD and
RUMOR are the methods of THE DIRECTOR.

ATHENE has never soiled his lips, as
A soldier, she is THE GODDESS OF WISDOM,
And CRAFTS. He has entered by her and…

ATHENE {on a skafold of the Heavens}

The ALIENIST desires to enter PROMETHEUS;
Espial as a portion of ZEUS'S reign.
Thought control is his method, Word Choice
Is mimicked guess techniques. The DIRECTOR
In the crown of heaven appears and
Espouses your FREE CHOICE. FREEDOM
Is this guy's will, THE WILL OF HEAVEN.

Mankind is what? An ANOPNPOS? I like
The form, excuses me, the door is rapped.
PROMETHEUS it is you! I was fixing my hair
And dream of riches that the GODS offer.
DARLING your reason for entering?
This is the reason I know you are now SANE!
But you were not this way before. DARLING.

DELUSIVE HOPE

They have a CORPORATION for production of information.
At the computer sits the former conspirer, PARNASSIA.
The She-Communication-Propagandist would no longer visit
The Balaton. PROMETHEA who was recently elected to
The consul of the Deities, regretted the loss of financiers,
Had begun PRIVITIZATION and the INDIVIDUALIZATION.
There investments would be irredeemable if the Deutsch
Would be permitted to occupy the vacation area. Sebastian
Returned to PRAHA promptly, the day after the demonstrations
Re-elected an old government. This had been foretold years
Before in THE CASTLE MUSEUM. Now they would be free again,
The political patricians would better themselves even if they
Had HALLUCINATIONS.

Komrade lAvel's relative told me of how he had attempted
To make public the written theories of his new finances.
Mr. wAdar had published his speeches, and Mistress lvel
Wished to show the world that his region would DISTRIBUTE.
These theories which he had contributed in the former
Local jazz club, before THE AMERICANS had returned
Regional 'rock' and popular 'ELECTRONIC' music.
He convinced THE LEADERSHIP that the Americans had indeed
Invented 'rock and roll' and that this was only legal
And would destroy all INTERNATIONAL ORDER. The Sofiet
Leaders thought this of minor importance to have
And international crisis over the music of the dissident,
WHITE TRASH.

The capitalist laughed that this fool in the Sofiet leadership
had such a good heart that he believed that all religious people
were like his grandmother.

PROMETHEUS

I will not accept ZEUS position.
I have deceived THE DIRECTOR, his
Preference, skeleton and lard, and
His VENGEANCE for distaste of Man.
From you, ATHENE, sweet child I
Have learned what was expelled.
THE ARTS, and SCIENCES from his
Crown.

The servile judge from the heavens
Has decreed that MANKIND is unfit,
And we must be rid of their kind.
Zeus has refused to permit Fire
From the CHARIOT OF HEAVEN, I must
Ignite and deliver the flame from
This SUN. Thank you, my dear,
Now I will repay your favor.

SICKNESS {oN a Skafold of Mal{ice}.

I AM A CHRISTIAN, A JEW, AND A CATHOLIC.
I AM SICKNESS. I have varnished man's nature
I deteriorate his body, weaken it.
Vomit, I am NAUSEA and pain is my sorrow.
Joy is my heart, sadism my mortality.
Disappointment ruins our intestines, infest
With microorganisms, my spine, my brain.
Pastel pale is my color, menstrual, my tint.
SELFLESSNESS for belief in this gild religion.
True faith is our ultimate treasure, our idol.
We are DISEASED, we are pretty, or riffraff.

I AM AILING, since my operation I have not been

Well. They have now a new name, to recreate new
Funds. IMMUNITY and PREPETUATION enhance WEALTH.
We can afford to dissect, to ATATOMIZE your Creed.
We can assure you of worst health. Your AGENT has
Contacted us, you are in fine hands with us too.
Your MINISTER has also called, the driver of the VEHICLE
Was KILLED. I have been not informed of this until
Your release. The new leader of the government
Needs samples of your blood type, your URINE,
And a specimen of ejaculation; no; discharge,
Is the present polite phrase. PRESIDENT GORBAKN
Has not ordered this, the new leader will.

Your BEHAVIOR has caused this tragic accident, this
Statement is designed, by the SENATOR, to test your
Loyalty, but I was asleep and I don't remember.
Was I this person? Was I in an accident, was this
My doing. My God! Magog! MR. SCRUB was murdered,
And he is free. He has never harmed anyone.
He broke every LAW OF GOOD MANNERS.
I was the daughter of a physician,
It is not possible to be ERRATA.

INSANITY

These are my INSTRUMENTS: bribery, and slander.
We dissect insight, knowledge and replace it,
With experience; labor, idleness, slumber,
Sabotage, ignorance, mimicry, postulation,
Edginess, presumption, and misperception.
WE SURROUND ourselves with mouths, teeth,
Hair, silence, smell, disease, viruses,
Germs, filth, reconstruction, fibers,
Used-machinery, voiceless speech,
Whining and idiocy.

LAWS are dollars, poverty is status,
Judgement is hearing, harassment, homicide,
Vice, riches are debt, wealth, money. TIME
A journal, propaganda sheet, entertainment,
Liquor, smoke, nausea, aspirins, deterioration,
Strength, medicine, abstinence, prohibition,
Rights, violation of self, treaties, agreements,
Poisons, mindlessness, destruction, boldness,
Dirt, exile, homelessness, debate, legislation,
Candor, deception, filibuster, film, and incest.

I am REGROWTH; premature ripeness; frigidness;
Stillness, regression, triumph, involvement.
I was a MONARCH; a leper; regeneration, and
Instruction. You are espial, attendance, and
Enthusiasm, gazing, reporting, mediation,
participation, worship, listening, yet realization.

You got it, PROMETHEUS is old fashion,
And before my parents speak, OLD AGE
Will climb the skafold; so for now
And a little later TELEMANN. Bring
Forth the legislation.
The poet never completed this poem
And was tortured into writing PROMETHEUS.
I had hope to fool him, but he has spoken
To me, his confident, that this poem
Is ENVIRONMENTAL. The poet has control
Of the district, he has been there a few
Times; and he is very liberal, you know
He doesn't permit anyone to do anything
Productive. So he has put this aside
And the FOURTEENTH VENGEANCE
is warming up.

FINALLY, THAT famed portion, which lead
the poet near the state of permanent
exaltation. Why not spend a little time
in the barracks? Why fight for Poetry, he
has reminded us? MY GODDESS, fight for
the politik; For if religions
are good, POETRY IS GREATER, all that is
right, all that is unjust, all else is crime.

DIRECTOR! Politiks is vulgar,
A prerequisite
For the accumulation of wealth.
Necessary, for the regression
Of the PARNASSIAN homeland,
The nameless fatherland.

    So the poet,
Set aside this great work,
Which someday he will return to,
I am sure. For now, be illuminated
That we will alter his imprint!
Get ready, THE FOURTEENTH appearith.
    A former English Maidenhead.
Thank you, Thank you.

The skafold of Mal{ice}.

We are not old,   we are OLD AGE.
Weakness and   power command.
Our voice is   not heard, yet
when we speak   meaninglessness
become the defense   of others.

Pretenders   and felons
Announce and   emulate their   preconception
While they   rationalize   their notions.
Their lack   of feelings.

MORANS MINIC

Discussion   and debate,

  simulate   advertisement.

While we rest   and concern   ourselves

With pastimes   and contemplation.

Their plans and   our diversions,

their manipulations, extortion's,   and blackmails

frighten the past,   and our trivial   intents.

We relive   and remake,   preventing

creations.   How may we   prolong life?

May we be awakened   into quietness

And serenityor stirred   into discontent quietude?

May we not sleep   or be crushed   beneath

    our marrow!

May we not frailly conceive   nightmares of possessions.
TIME must be made present,   the end must be enlightened
And seen, passed on.   pushed forward.
STIFLED!

After years of similitude   and habitual manner
hindsight conquers and   perpetuates the estate
against political and   grins us into boredom
from distractions.
EXCITEMENT in tranquility   and exultation, frenzy
ADDICTION TO ACHIEVEMENT   AND COMMUNITY
PROPAGATION.

Oneness and power tyrannize   and UPLIFT minute
distinctions.
commands and childish dances
grow into fashion with them
enliven and perpetuated   forgotten relived restrengthen.

Youth empowered by us,   old age, not stifled or
hindered. We no longer   conduct or orchestrate,
we construct, reorganize,
replace, and resent   observation, learning.

Contribute to control   and destroy
so political arrant
can render wastefulness   productive
disruptions   and violence
to render potholes   of red tape
and experiments   impolitely

HOSPITALS threaten us,
and torture our children
ruin our saving,
squandering lielessness.

We still perform our daily chores
what we are told and imagine
enlivened
buried in dependence and
                  inherited.

The grand cities anointed and
stimulation.

The remembrances of our forefathers
secrets not revealed emotions

When will we guess or desire
profit?

 We could offer an ELIXIR in
insight
thrills and chill our souls.
striving in flesh to ignore
merely to mend a button,
is drugged stimulation

There are no spirits and ghost
transcended in mind process
and thoughts. We will no longer
we will hide forever! We will
disbanded,
but may return to this theme,
There is no eternity or afterlife
We rule while others reign
succession.

        and perceive
PROMISES fulfilled

re-enlightened northward

suppression at

revealed in silence
risen and repeated daily.

immorality perpetuated

health perpetuated in

neo-spirits, non-beings
any paradise or heaven.
or clean a dish, forever
of repeated observation.

only lifelessness

      be old age
be forgotten, lost,

yet we are OLD AGE.
      we are OLD AGE.
      in triumph and

FALSEHOOD

Today my follows, I have   heard falsehood.
As I was at the shopping mall,
an agent of falsity was silent
She is the MINISTER OF INQUIRY.
He is in manservant against   the law
He defies the unimaginative,   they summons
liberty of thought reading.   she submits
ANNOYANCE diverts his attraction,
He lust without feeling or   involvement
Now a pamphlet of marcescent   has been published

People walk the streets in pairs,   another man
plods along the sidewalk,
              two women chat
I have forgotten what it is like   to be a host
to worship my citizens, I remember   once I was in old
age,
once I was in sickness. the world   abandon me not
it was at my shelter, my pleasure.   my clothing
ruined.

THE ARENA OF MARS: a junk car,   a red chariot.

a file neglected, Yet I was not   in the present,
nor the past, hereafter.
I am not the author of this rhyme,   these creatures
are salvation, for now I will   live forever.
That I remembered the hope   that I will return.
DEATH has been defeated,   Falsehood reigns; transformation
into Vice

You have forgotten, I spoke to myself,   our ministry observes a woman.

[descending the skafold:] [Passion ascends the Banns…]

From above the heavens, we hear the underworld.
We have demolished and wrecked; Let us return to those
Words which you, my parishioners, were conceived without…

LABOUR [skafold of the world]

Last night I was raw from EXPERIMENTATION,
For twenty years I have not been able to practice
My profession. Wages are my accumulation of PRIVACY.
Everything is a lie, the hope of opportunity bestowed
Upon the advantaged, those who are fortunate to believe
Work without a profession. I myself have followed the path
of the yard, which I have purchased. I am weary of servitude.
I have escaped the mule road of RELIGION, and the highway
CAPITALISM. Now I lay in a chair and relax and study…

I receive the appreciation of happiness, the enemy that
Prays upon generation, and tortures everyone, robs them. This
Is servitude, the HOSPITAL of the martyred COMMANDER. The
Demonic hideous PHANTOMS, the morbid
methods of MECHANICS.

HEALTH is their knowledge, LOVE learning, death their TENDER,
Raw words and bribery, stupidity and misinformation; their food
Poison, torn clothing; dollars paper, and false collection.
TV (television), sports, drugs, liquor, medicines, magazines,
Preconceived mental perversions, a decrepit community.
Whose correctness is inhumanity. Yet I LABOR, am not their employer
Neither correctness is INHUMANITY. I LABOR,
the tool of their   Inoculation.

THE DIRECTOR OF THE NATION desires a robust environment
He has switched health care supplements

After a reign of chaos, it has taken us one year
To enact our program, fairness for your generation.
I have informed my press, at our latest conference.
That we will lift the embargo on our brethren in the high land.
There the palm trees create warm weather and dry snow.

THE DIRECTOR OF HE STATE

An actor attempted to enter the home of the great Imposter!
As usually he was loaded, smoked legal methane; and had
OLD AGE with children and potato chips; he also solicited
The fired and disgraced writer; of course, this is established
That he can neither write or spell or read; Jeef s his name.
JEEF dragged to infiltrate the atmosphere, to sanctity the new
Electrical system as the promotion plugger, labored a weapon
Fruitfully for the return of the heroine of the NATION.

In disguise, as usual, she was accosted by intruders
She would of course reveal to the community the enlightened
Opinion of Jeef's mother's OBSESSION. Her dear son
Would one day save the community of violence and
Terrorism. The Jeef would not permit this and began
An alinement to incarcerate this perpetuator
Of world tranquility. The town failed to relocate
Five dollars paid for Jeef's next visitation; January
Prover profitable toward the attainment of the sought
For elimination of unrest,

Years of improvement by out ladies in the fifties building
Proved deteriorating to the determent of the SIA; unfortunate.

He had not been permitted to restrict his dogs to the location
Therefore, the though the elks in New Jerzip, repair the

Azinc-layer, as depicted in the flop film which Sfed
Imitated about failed impersonators guardian.

Demolition by prayer of the building.

The jar

My words kill this person who ordered the alteration of this speech.

PASSION

And you have slept, and not liked?
My avidity in you, now you do not?
PROMETHEUS, I do not shape your appeals
I do not speak? You must! I use you? No.
We memorized this automobile on decapitalized tv
We now must do this, unlike them, at leisure.
they will never overturn our fraternization.
For what good is it to me; I have now learned
This from TV. You father, ZEUS, told you of this.
We women; PROMETHEUS, we have no passion.
Only PLEASURE. I will try this on you: you like this.

Yes, perhaps yes, what is your name? Spell what?
Speak what? Don't talk, you like this. Why do you
Not finish. PASSION, why do you not finish?
Is it too much for you? SWEETWOMEN, it is not!
Why do you turn your neck; is it not your neck more?
Beautiful? No, don't turn. Do smile. For ATHENE
Loves me, and hates you. Yes. Now do you JUSTITA,
Please.

Why answer you? Figure it out, look at me, look at me.
Why must I look at you? Must I touch you? Will you slit

Their wrist. My pleasure? Will you? Now you are fine.
My veins feel better, your bust, feel on palms
Teach me, how you like it. Will you stay, before FOURTEEN.
My birthday is tomorrow, will you stay? Will you.

No, I must? not. This is passion. You are pleasurable.
PASSION. I must be in Sophia. In FOURTEEN. Then to home?
Yes, then to VENGENCE. Call me. Why not finish? Why not finish?
My number, paper, write. Call me. Finish, Return when?
For police, protection, money? Please to Sophia.
Problem. Pleasure. I go. I finish. No pay me.

                              VICE

My name is VICE. It is a nice name.
The religious slander me. I am a nice
Figure. VICE is the means with which
POETRY, and it's immortal increment
Pulchritudian Parnassian EPOETEST
Eminent and eliminate the virtues
Of the illiterate. Prostitution
Is my finest virtue. Buffoonery
Is my second, I love only
Self-indulgence,I only deprive
The religious of this marriage.
For their corruption is donation,
Contribution. I am fine, I am good.
I am best. I don't wish to propagate.
I wish to wed. I like enjoyment,
Celebrity. I am, THE VICEROY of PLEASURE.
The initiator of PASSION, the creator
Of theology: the employment of ethics.

the death of the pretenders
THE THIRTEENTH DOWERY
PORTION THIRTEEN

THE DEMOCRACY
OF THE

COMMUNIST LEFT

THIS IS NOT A PUBLIC
DOCUMENT.

THE DICTATORSHIP OF THE COMMUNIST LEFT

Now MY ENEMIES, we have cognate
RELATIONAUTHORITY with negy(four) regions
Southern New Jerzip, Bohemia, Slovakia,
Oberachsen, Thuringia, Magyarorsza,
and Russia.

   **** small part of new cognitive notation; developed since 1992.****

With ultimate MYTHOS and GEOpoliTICAL
HerALDic achievement in these areas,
POWER is THE FORCE of evolutionary creative esthetic pleasure.
The more COGENCY, the more pleasure. via
the appetite, in a power ridden of
THE CAPITALIST, only through power will we
cRUSH the tyRANy of US CAPITALISM;
through aggrandized AUTHORITY,
have we begun to Obtain ultimate joy,

pleasure, emotions, and natural feelings.

In a WORLD 'DEAD' from US Capitalism,
only the methods of mechanization are
Capable TO REPRODUCE adequate 'COPYTEST'
extermination pest EXaltaTION.
MY ENEMIES, for their friends scorn and crave correction(prison)
but 'PRISON OF THE MIND' is a mere sufficient sentence
to increase emotions.
Why not release their EMpatHY in a cell wall of LEPROSY,
not illiterate enough for passive femin (TV) TELEVISION
receptive perversion.
The Xtain age reverts to the age of CIVILIZATION.

SECURITY TRIAL

THE UNCORRECTED (those not in want of,
as opposed to those NAZI criminals(
THE CATHOLIC NAZI, the 'GOOD PERSON';
which was exposed in the ANTI-SELF
(the NAZIJEW replacement
Mythical manic imagination)
The 'respected person'
In the 'poet's'
poem 'THE ANTI-CHRIST'.

We have lived with the deTERiorATing
cuSToms of the reLIGious, especially
the catholics, jewish, protestant, and fundamentalist PRESTigitATION.
They will not be sent to the colleges
for the religious, the true religions
should contemplate 'LIFE HEREAFTER'.
The real, CONTEMPORARY WORLD, for
the 'SICK' entombed past of infertile
ritual; we will have a living ceremony, for
ANGUISH OF PERIPATETIC

centuries we have been tortured:
torture the 'BLINDFOLD' goddess.

The 'TOOTH' of REVENGE, then we will
begin counterattack, retaliation.
We have demoNstrated our poWer, in SUD
NEW JERZIP, my enemies;
To all of Friends, Banks, Distributers - ships, and leaders have fallen
At our wills, and our friends, will receive THE CREDIT for this work.

We are THE SYMBOLS and THE INSTRUMENTS of
POWER, MY ENEMIES AND COMRADES;
We are THE VOICE OF REALITY, the real
world of the artist magnificent laughter
For REAlity is what we diCTate and disTort in the misBELieVes and
MISPERCEPTIONS of our dearest friends, MY
ENEMIES AND COMRADES, we live in
ECSTASY and AGGRANDIZED PLEASURE,
in threat of enterprise and retaliation,
Our friends shall have toTAL freEdom, and live in myTHical world
OF THE CAPITALIST.

INSANE IGNORANCE, we will allow all respect, and certification.
They will never even PERceive that they aRe even free oF oUr ridicule
power control, OUR FRIENDS, are indeed the
HOMO SAPIENS level of animal nature.
They will remain as mammals;
or domestic creatures, free and vocal.
This is THE METHOD of satisfying THE CAPITALIST.
TRIAL BY ERA

WOMEN AS THE WILL TO POWER

I have spoken of the work of the greatest philosopher,
Friedrich Nietzsche 'THE WILL TO POWER'.
In comrade Stephen Sweigart's poem 'THE TRIUMPH OF DEATH',
The poet quotes a passage from this book
'ART AS THE WILL TO POWER';
                    To cause

THE 'NEW' COMMUNIST,
hetrosapiens.

We may breed unproperly, capitalist genetics
and Christian genetics created AIDS virus.
Must be ignored, Christian MALFEASANT BREEDING HABITS;
Abandoned when THE CHRISTIAN first began to form groups.
They were all men, Jesus of Nazareth,
Ignored and mistreated WOMEN;
excluding them from their 'Gay Men's' RELIGIOUS
Of UNARTISTIC unCrEaTive INTEKLeCTual huMan siMPletons"
Who by means of DISSENT PROPAGATION
and preaching which replaced
Natural ReliGiOn which is conCeRNed with
'LIFE' , NoT LIFE AFTER ' DEATH'
As oPPoSed to THE CHRISTIAN mens'clubs manners (destructive).
CREATIVE ARTIST create and build
CIVILIZATION, with natural vigor.

IN THE CIVILIZED WORLD , Greece and Rome,
WOMEN were aesthetically pleasing
and enjoyable and a source of wisdom;
anyone who studies myth and art;
Knows that THE JUDAIC-CHRISTIAN
ORDER is repulsive, sadistic, cruel
and, unsacred, inhuman, otherworldly, uncreative.
Think of Stephania, Diana, Susan, Josephine, Mary,
Clarice, Gabriella, Robin, Laura, Vida.
Realize the 'SICKNESS' of Mary and
Magdeline, sick women, MY GOD.

How horrible is THE CHRISTIAN WAY OF
LIFE, only artist have subverted
and destroyed all that is degenerate in Judeo-Christian mankind.
'LIFE' all art history proclaims and slowly reinstates 'MYTH'.
THE REVOLUTIONARY PROCESS AND DEVelopMENTal
GENERATION of THE HUMAN SPIRIT
CREATIVITY replaces MASOCHISM, a
hateful stage of evolution; denial
Of anything but the END of 'LIFE'; LIFE
AFtER DEATH; THE IDOLATRY. . .
cont. .

THE PRESIDENT OF THE COMMUNIST LEFT. .

MOUTHS OFF BRILLANT SIA PLANS. . . . . . .
About killing THE DIRECTOR and THE FOUNDER
OF THE COMMUNIST LEFT. . .
THE FORMER DEMOREPUB PRESIDENT,
and female torture expert
beLIEves that he is really MSS. FLOSET
and is willing to conTEMPlate
ChANGing hir seX if he can also REPLACE the dictator and founder,
our enemy the 'POET', who disapproves the
intrusion of WAR ZONE 13.

CAPITALIST AMERICA must remain inquest
FLOSST DECLARES; We must murder
The poet and founder of THE COMMUNIST
LEFT, I am the President
This poet has ruined Komrade Korter and Komrade Koetan. . .
We know that THE COMMUNIST have flourished in Neu Jerzip. . .
We must ELIMINATE and REPLACE
THE COMMUNIST LEADERS
Even if it creates a BRAIN DRAIN loSs; we
must supplant all COMMUNIST
We are good AMERICANS , we are CAPITALIST and CHRISTIANS.

me Jikail Flost, the pRESIDENT OF uNETeD SToTes OF jErZIP.
THIS FaMILY OF preter-PReTEnDERS AND CRIMINALS
ARE A DETRIMENT OF THE HUMAN RACE
THEY MUST BE WIPED FROM THE FACE OF THE EARTH
'IT IS JUST TO

'MURDER'
COMMUNIST!

THE PHILOGIST ENJOYS:

BUT FOR ME THE ONLY JUSTICE IS
mILTON WAS A GREAT POET, AND
A GREAT SCIENTIST, THERE WAS NEVER
ANY SIR ISAAC; ONLY A TORTURED
GREAT HUMAN BEING, JOHN MILTON.

THE MANSLAUGHTER BY THE RELIGIOUS ELEMENT.

TAX - - SEPARATION OF CHURCH AND STATE
The religions of NeU JeRZIP
poison and murder all non-donational citizens
unlike religions of other states;
in which the religious are wealthy.
Through the eradication of the 'CREATIVE' element
toilsome labor - - the joy of 'LIFE AFTER DEATH'
the learning of the bi-sexual mode of moral reproduction.

JULIETTA TRIPS TO GREECE.

Last we heard 'JULI' was greECed up for a few weeks
She got tired of singing and calling Sebastian
Her voice needed a vacation
Sebastian never had enough money;
but greECed up JULIETTA produced LIPNAILS on TV
(TRANSVESTITE TELEVISION) she reversed her piGment.
Paid $50,000; her TENNIS snicker collateral
Then she was offered by Mary Klakiy to fill in
When she needed a fiX; her hubby was a CANdiDATe
To be the LAST Lady for a day was her kBg drEAm
Her ouTFIT was prePared over a period of fifteen
Years at a cost of HER COMRADES EnsLAveMEnT.
Actually though her conTerParts in PiNslytania
Paid much dearer, as the commonwhiil LOTTO puffed
dEAcoN balls with symbols the average TV birdBrain
At the CaSino Regulatory Board of ENCROACHMENT.

THE SPORTSMAN ABSTRACT CONTACT BRIBERY.

Call PROktolokist and at the BaGLes Net
You can learn to call signals and memorize
That air balls and jocks reproduce unaWareness
Of value to A CAPITALIST RELIGIOUS SYSTEM.
That MANUFACTURES transFormatioal and dEAcon
Possession of one's body with riTes and
Programed ANCHOR installment of buddy fayMent.
Xtain friendship relationships; voices
Restricted TO A few individuals creates
A psychological xtain deRANGement situation
That prevents MASS COMMUNICATION via ONESELF.

In the 'LIVING' environment; to restrict
The individual from coMMuNal activity is indeed
The method of the xtain CAPITALIST STATE control
 DERANGEMENT APPARATUS which is designed and built
To preVent an noTed tO middle age etc.

MRS. GULLIBLE POLICES A STATUS WOODCOCK.

A few NON -LITERATE political CAPITALIST STATUS POLICE
who licked ROOKO roll in THE INTERNATIonal ponfake
and whent donnies soUthern kAMPferd pesTUtent
to pill A STATE POOPER wife's yphaLAtic egina.
For a few bucks for a Kewford Ed for their kauGHTers
TaRnoKry wig plant in the Heart institute
POISON every THIRD PARTY citizen and make them fellow
HOMO SAPIENS (exual)while we humans must exist.

Ms. KIDER and Ms. JEMINK must be geromoniously HARMED.
They cannot continue to sacrifice principles
For STATUS and APPEARANCE, and more than
THE DISTRIBUTION WEALTH can not exist with
The CAPITALIST RELIGIOUS ELEMENT in power.
Our residence, our presence, our SACRED
no church, cathedral , no clergyman
Can turn back time as we of THE COMMUNIST LEFT .

NO ONE can produce GREAT ART without benefit
UNFORTUNATELY, THE RELIGIOUS ELEMENT is totally
Responsible for MANKIND'S DEGENERATION, INTERFERENCE
With NATURE and it's DESTRUCTION, is the product
Of the religious , not necessarily THE BELIEVER.
INTERFERENCE with art, or SUBJECTION of the ARTIST
Is the most vile act of AN INHUMAN and DEGENERATE
RACE OF CRIMINALS.
My residence contains the LiVes
Of the greatest 'BEINGS' and creatures, my home
In possessed of FOURTY-THREE years of HATE
of the VIOLATORS OF distortion, lies, propaganda

MIND CONTROL, and the great RESISTANCE to the
Most EVIL and DEGENERATE ELEMENT, the people that
Eradicate all who CREATE, and build CIVILIZATION.

ARTIST BUILD, the NAZI destroy.
COMMUNIST build,
Political Parties destroy.
All Nazi's are 'SICK'.

INTERFERENCE WORD PLANT 555.

PROGRAMED IDIOT 56
THE POET PROGRAMS THE WORD CHOICE
OF THE NON-LITERARY ELEMENT
PRE-PLANT WORD CHOICE SELECTION
GATHERING FACTORS
mIND CONTROL MEDICATION ERADICATION
SIMPLIFICATION REJECT.
EVOLUTIONARY SEED WORIFICATION
// RACE GROWTH OF THE POET
THE POETS ELECTORAL ACCEPTANCE
PERCEPTION OF THE RACE

LOCAL GENERATION AND
ENLIGHTENMENT OF THE POET.
SOUTHERN NEW JERSEY AMERICAN NAZI) FORMAL
(EDUCATION UNLETTERED ILLITERACY
PROGRAM HYSTERIA 6666 / SOUND YEARS MOVIE MIMIC
EDUCATION CHANCE / MINGLING EFFECT REALIZATION
PRODUCT LIST 4 / MERCHANDISING LIST 3
COGNITION SEED WORD RECALL RELEASE 23
JASON THE ARGONAUT; THE 'TEETH'
THAT FOUGHT CAPITALISM.

THE DEITY OF HE SUN

CAPITALISM IS THE CREATION OF THE
RELIGIOUS ELEMENT OF MANKIND
THE RELIGIOUS CREATED CAPITALISM-
~~TO ENSLAVE MANKIND FURTHER~~
ONLY IN THIS POEM; THE COMMUNIST LEFT POEM
BY THE POET, STEPHEN SWEIGART,
AFTER TWENTY-FIVE YEARS OF SILENCE
DO WE CLEANSE OUR HANDS OF THIS GREAT SIN?
WHY NOT TEACH EVERYONE?????? HOW I WRITE!
WHY NOT FAWN MY BODY TO DEATH;
YOU RELIGIOUS FRIENDS
BUT KNOWLEDGE IS THE THEME OF REALITY
ALL GREAT POETRY REFLECTS REALITY; COMMUNISM
AND DECEPTION; THE END OF RELIGIOUS CAPITALISM!

CHOXTINA IS PLEASED TO DISCOVER!
CHOXTINA IS PLEASED TO DISCOVER!

AT A LATER STAGE of THE CRIMINAL
government INVESTIGATION;
THE POET IS sHot with raDIAtion, aftEr fifTteen yEaRs
oF THE STATUS POLICE denial of their KriMinal methods.
'CHIXT' is ecstatic because the STATUS POLICE weaken all
OppoNents (eXual), I ofTen REMEMBER hir speAking,
'How every COMMUNIST should starve;
and hoW eVEry COMMUNIST
Must 'INJECTED' with bacteria, larvae, and viruses'.
JerZiY BRIWN was her largest VicTIMizer, he was once
A tranPOLical but became 'NAZI' in a months TIME.
It was neceSSary she remembers to RESTriCT expreSSion
THE STATUS POLICE allowed TOTAL FREEDOM, which could
onLy be reaLIZed with the maNuFACTers of these wEAPons
of RADIATION SICKNESS; theReFore it was neCESSary
to MoVe the COMPUTER SCREEN to a non-DiRECT loCATion.
So that finally a FEMINIST STATUS rEALized that finally its' method
Of seXual expeSSion, THE STATUS POLICE thought it was
A vaLid alTERnative to rePROducTion.

STEPHANIA HOOKS AND INFECTS WOMEN III

mY gOD, SHe iS One oF my goDs, a hOOker Forever
Everyday I dream of her sexual ENCOUNTERS with
Women, MOST whom she has inFlicTed with 'SIAS'.
A new 'SICKNESS' invented when she was discovered
To poSSeSS a few cut off 'RICKS'; how esTaTic
I was IN her REVELATION men loved to FAWN them.
My, God, she is in a 'RUSH' to all who BEHOLD her
The priest LOVE 'LIPNAILS' and the mInIsters
Realize she is a SERVANT in their guise of HATE
For it was she that TAUGHT us, 'RELIGIOUS ARE EVIL'
Her FISH BOWL has SPERM TREATMENT Test Samples
In order to improve Her rAce; the race of hOOkers
DISCRIMINATION is never ACCEPTABLE and we NEVER
PROSECUTE LEGALLY; for it cost the government money
Very few ATTORNEYS accept this FACT OF LIFE.

JULIETTA FORTUNA, AND STEPHANIA BANKRUPTS.

The purity of Godrealla INFLICTS me with madness
Such a beautiful VESTAL creature brings anguish
Her breast have finally grown and my duties are though
No longer will I be able to behold THE BEAUTY of her body
Like the 1500 women whom I have natured unwilling.
STEPHANIA'S purity as a 'PRIESTESS' evades me
She was hopelessly condemned to LACK OF PROTECTION.
And as always she was assigned to me, this burden
Makes me sick with love, weak with words and expression
Yet JULIETTA is sexual, alive and impure?
My goD, BEAUTY is everything with her, emotion replaces
Truth, why should I love truth, why not, IMMiSSioN
Of SEXUAL PLEASURE is FAR BEYOND ANY TRUTH.

TEST TUBE REPRODUCTION PRODUCT 5

THE SPANISH CONQUISTADORS 'MURDER'.
'RAPE', AND 'POISON' NEW JERZIP.

The 'SpiK' mammas cann't control their 'TITS' spit
ANTI-COMMUNIST PROPAGANDA
in mother tongue of the church
A fat spanish mamma presence 'kills' any New Jerzip.
The very nature of this race is OBJECTionable
The CONQUISTIZATION by the great rocco roller
Gerqip Parcia with $34,000,000 in 'intake' and
'MURDER' and 'APE' of thousand more, a good church
GoER and a 'PURE' spanish catholic dissident
HAS his 'DEATH' on earth, immortal in the hearts
Of children, whom help ADDict with ROCK.
Whose lives he ruined with his addiction to the intake
That subverted and distributed drugs via an entertainment
System which controls THE GOVERNMENT by illegal (legal)
DESTRUCTION of the children which the conquistadors intake.

THE 'MAD' VALT FIRMIB DESTROYS MANKIND WITH NAZI
ANTI-POETICS AND MISINTERPRETATION'

THE LOST GENERATION he achieves his ALTRUISTIC plans fail.
THE 'MANIA' to expose all who prevented his consumerism.
He sells good to a NEW FASHION, every
year as a good 'PETTY' socialist.
MONEY may be created and labor out of fashionable comodies.
A new MAIL BOX creates work, a new car
creates work and feeds people,
ART is something to be stolen, sabotage
and impersonation, and replaced
HIS DAUGHTER could not even take A
COMPLIMENT, after she met A TAXI DRIVER;
WHO ENLIGHTENED her to the glory of
abandoned years ago, AS OF VALUE.

The 'MAD MAN' is unpoetic and naïve,
he believes riches rule the world;
rather than UNLEARNING and KNOWLEDGE,
he has no understanding of valueless
information ridicule as cheap why not influence your minds.
Why not ALTRUISTIC NON-POETIC influence
of unlearning and knowledgeless.
The real absurd theater of 'POSITION' as opposed to enjoyment. .

THEFT TO ACHIEVE WHAT? Riches, slavery
of dependance; destruction of human
enlighten creative advancement as opposed to unnecessary fashionable
reproduction . THE MIND OF A PERFORMER

and A MANUFACTURER which ruin the very
worth of creative evolutionary advancement
not achieved through preying
to fawn and flatter, debt ingratiating rather than build and design.
Food comes from sanitarily primarily and not theft.

THE PRESIDENT OF THE CAPITALIST.

THE GREATEST
PRESIDENT OF
THE CENTURY
That THE OWNER of
THE COMMUNIST LEFT
of THE POLITICAL
BRAIN TRUST, that
demonstrated his
abilities to deal
JRQEY BRIW, the
warped mastermind
The NAZI methods
have altered, but
of in a recent election, and is a

to the NAZI movement.
He has failed
THE COMMUNIST
ARE defeating and

struggling with the
DEMOREPUB
(who still does not
accept the view)
'fact' THE INFANTILE
DISORDER means
When the truth of the
NAZI deception

has today admitted publicly

is now accepted in the ranks

the poet himself, has finally

with the NEO-
NAZI director,
IDIOT of the NEO-
NAZIS TAKEOVER
the mastermind has been deposed

declared senile infantile
embarrassment
to accept the reality that

reversing THE STATE
CAPITALIST

Anti-Communist HYSTERIA
and HYENAS
is revealed to all concerned.

MR. NOBODY RUINS THE PIAMS OF
THE ANTI-COMMUNIST.

THE ANTI-COMMUNIST masterminds don't want MR. NOBODY
to ruin the plams for the denomenfication(clation).
MRS.TERESA TRANSBUY is the plannational intelligence,
She is considered the greatest tramsklan member of the world.
NO LONGER are communist on THE PAND
LIST, no longer are the Clofake
on THE PLAN LIST. He now has a new
'CONTRACT' in Florida with the at helitic
TELEFON sales strategic usuric transfer of idea's to put ateletic
supporters
back in last place, MARRY into a 'BASSBALL
CAMP' inorder to remaster mind
in a method better than old grandpa Adolf,
THE STATE CAPITALIST methods
TO ANIMALIZE all but the truthful members
of the NAZI PARTY, get it straight
Msss.Terri is a hell of a homosexual cunt,
she purchased at Habi's expense
For Habi wants to hilp women become 'bassball' legend.
WOMEN have reach THE LEVEL OF EXISTENCE equal to 'birth'.
now they are able to wear ATHLETIC
SUPPORTERS on their mouths.
SELF-DEFENSE (LIFE ON EARTH)
VERSUS 'LIFE HERE AFTER'
THE GREAT GOG in a deceptive machine
of glory and eternal strength
At the age of puberty the great plan enfolded before as the young

CHILD wrote a poem about THE SNOW
at the request of his once great
father. Through time and winter the
CATHOLIC NAZI assassinations and
murders 'THE SILVER CHARGER' of
poison, replacement, the last attempt
(the feedback interrupting inspiration) (the
microphones of criminal activity)
of the religious to CONSPIRE and
MANSLAUGHTER, as ordered by the former
CONMAN in his rejermandered district,
inorder to regain funds for a lost
cult of the extermination of 'CREATIVE', the rich, the wealth of a few
to feed a small mass to use as AN EXTERMINATION
SERFS of THE VESTMENTS.
The JUDAIC-CHRISTIANS destroyed Rome
the same way they have seized power
In PINNloVania, Nuo GeoRRei, and Nuo KoRko, destroying
'THE CREATURE' and replacing through SECRET
SERVICE procedures and signed forced by weapon
agreements to obtain office. The poet again poisoned and his poem
once sent into registration was printed and won an award, but the
ROMAN CATHOLIC dictator switch his name
to the future women, that was designated
to replace him, he never entered the contest, because he then received
a low mark, to establish that he had no
literary talents, except in solitude
where his thoughts could in the future be changed
into to unlearned indoctrination.

Once it was permitted to buy books or order
and the poet when 'threatened'
by the NAZICATHOLICS youth leader, began
to accumulate his books, shoplifting
procedures at election times tortured him when it was discovered he had

built his own library over twenty some years, starvation, harrasement, so the conception of the 'poet' verses the 'CARDINAL' of the catholic NAZI (Roman Catholic equals <NAZI> national socialist).

THE ELECTED COMMUNIST 'LANNER' OF THE CENTRAL COGRATE OF NEW JERZIP.

The great traffic construction: TRAFFIC AS THE WILL TO POWER.
Now that the great manufacturer THE
COGNATE PLANNER has inactivated
The nihilistic sextrotary since he and governerd are too rich
In combarison the COGNATE PLANNING
DIRECTORSHIP uncoordinated by
the soyialist director, and the TRAFFIC PATE
THE director and old friend of the HOLLYBOWL SYSTEM
or the excellent PEaNET PLANTATION OWNER
we try less harder, less work (NEW JERZIP WORKS).

THE TRAFFIC PATE embarrsed the freeloaders by working too hard.
The PLANNER and SOYIALIST DIRECTOR
loathe and the SEXTROTARY
and other unnamed BIG SHOTS at the
descint of the GIVERNESS herself
who beenivolently loathe all useless PRODUCTION
and CONTRABANN all
but CREATIVE ENJOYMENT AND PLEASURE
IN LASTING CONSTRUCTION and
this is indeed an excellent GIVERCEST, unlike the 'witch' from
the forestess realm (spoken of in portion tiz).

*****injured and beaten again and glasses
stolen, September 19, 1992*****

****SCIENTIST / gathering for PROCESS OF
ELIMINATION /   NICE VS. HORRIBLE STAGE 5 ****

ROOSEVELT WAS A HOBO
TRUMAN WAS A MADMAN

EISENHOWER WAS MURDERER
JOHNSON WAS A RAPIST

VENGEANCE FOURTEEN

THE REIGN OF GORE

JULIETTA APPROACHES 'THE POOR POETESS'

There has never been a women 'great poet'.
And I Julietta have been introduced to the Greatest of all Poetess.
I have approached you, magnificent poetess, with a jewel
which you should immortalize in verse, not rhyme.
Modernism is the tymp, the sweetheart of dalliance and demoiselle.
Recently, my child, I returned from the infirmary
with pellets and peppers searching for wine, my fiacre,
and her coachman, a man or a gladiator, I could not tell
for the little ladies were blabbering rather loud.

KUDUCTKI; ESQUIRE OF THE POLAKT KEMPt.

SLOWER the Nazi-Czech, spreading mukus undashed her duKet.
She is the wedlock of the wealthy linguistic at durkey,
BT KUTUKST, her dress he purchased in from her gay military
discount Krakow, the home of Ponntyvanio PTI. He paid
the Poluckless prostitute from Ponntyvania, sooner that
she has been promised to be the elected judicial servint
removes her pastors pennate and sells it to advertise about
sexual reproductive functions in the occupied territory
which ships apports filk with pineapple, she receives cigarettes

from her embasititude in to blow the Esquire cash to purchase.
creditcards in the Esquire favorite pin down doll.

The Poet is introduced to the poor poetess.

Dearest Stephen, in the far regions a crude little girl lives.
There you will be accosted by these uncouth women, Stephen,
I know of a fair little girl who has studied with us in Prague.
Beware of these women from the valley of the surgeons,
we have studied with this crude, but refined women from Slovakia
She lives in the valley of the surNeons, Stephen, I wish to wed.
These women from Soghia, are dirty, beware. They have two forms
Magnificence and lowliness humility, but this little girl from
must not be married when you meet her,
Stephen, she is very pleasurable
when you accept her marriage you will be taken down this magnificent
of marriage, for after marriage you will live lowly, she is the servant
of the lord of this nation. Thank you, you assure me you will seduce her.
You are our God for us now, Stephen if you do this, I will pray.
Now you will be able to feast with you, in a far greater manner.
You will defeat this inhuman lord, and they will be enslaved.
Darling, we can do nothing, against these women where you live.
They are, predators, not women, or even human. If you defeat this
Lord, we will be able to join your cause, and leave the DIRECTOR.
We will no longer be tortured by this great Capitalist DIRECTOR.

DISMEMBERMENT FIFTEEN

THE MORPHOLOGY OF STEPHANIA GODRIELLA;
THE BEATIFICATION OF BEAUTY.

The mamonization and sanctification of the
enmity of the Poet : Stephen Sweigart.

THINKING; REASONING; RETENTION; SALIVATION;
DISCRIMINATION; RELEARNING;
RECALL; RECOGNITION; REFECTION;
MEMORY; PERCEPTION; CONCEPTION;
LAUGHTER; EXPRESSIONS; SOUND;

COMMUNISTIC SELF-DEFENSE AGAINST USUARIC
CAPITALISTIC SYSTEM AND GOVERNMENT.

THE ADVANCE OF THE COMMUNIST LEFT MILITIA.

INFORM, ADMIT, DECLARE, TELL, ORDER
BROADCAST, PROPAGANDIZE.

9 781959 895701